"Hugging A Porcupine"
Reframing Customer Service

By Sidney C. Hurlbert and Francis M. Murphy

Illustrations by Edmond Madison

1

DEDICATION

*With the caveat that we both love our family and friends,
we dedicate this slim volume to our readers who,
by buying this book, have taken a step
to better serve their fellow humans.
Our hats are off to you!*

Customer Service Manual
By: Sidney C. Hurlbert and Francis M. Murphy

Great customer service springs from optimism, respect for others, and high expectations.

Introduction

Customers! Can't they be annoying? People in the trenches often tell us customers are more and more demanding each year. They say customers are inconsiderate, stubborn, difficult, and even rude.

Some principals of schools say "If it were not for those irritating students and parents, the school would be fun."

The problem is, without those annoying customers, none of us would be in business.

It is easy to blame the customer. But if these principals were honest, they'd also have to eliminate the teachers, staff, coworkers, the superintendent, and the Board of Education before schools would truly become fun for them. Chances are, however, these "customers" might have to remove the principal as well to have fun.

Fran's Mom used to say "I wonder about people except thee and me, and sometimes I wonder about thee."

Many teachers insist, "If only these two kids were gone, teaching this class would be great." Some researchers removed the two problem students from the teachers' classes.

What happened was that two more students rose to the top as the "problem students".

Groups seem to need a problem person. I call this the designated bum theory.' Every group needs a bum to blame when things go bad. In families, this person is often called the "black sheep". Perhaps we are safer when all the failures of the group can be blamed on the "bum."

After all, we don't have to be faster than the charging hungry bear, just faster than the person running alongside us so when the bear stops to eat him, we can get away.

It seems we all need to have a list of "problem people" among our customers. If it weren't for these "problem people", perhaps we might become the problem for our coworkers.

We can view all kinds of people as annoying: customers, family, coworkers, and our bosses. (Maybe, especially our bosses.) A college registrar did not enjoy students. He used to tell students that if they simply followed his written directions, that they would never have to see him to fix problems. "That," he said, "is what we are striving for."

Imagine striving to avoid your customers!

Many of us choose lives guided by our annoyance with other people. People can choose to be annoyed or to be delighted. Within tolerances, we are probably all surrounded by the same percentage of truly annoying people.

Yet some of us laugh, have fun, and celebrate, most days, while others mope and moan. It appears to be our choice. Some have lives focused on disappointments about other people. These people harbor low expectations. Research reveals that people will often rise or fall to the expectations that others have for them. So, these folks may be contributing to the problems they complain about.

Many experts in the field of customer relations assert there are three important reasons to focus on customer relations:

> **Positive customer relations improve the retention rate of customers. (This is true.)**

> **Positive customer relations lead to "word of mouth" advertising. (This is also true.)**

> **Positive customer relations can lead to greater profitability in the "for-**

profit" sector and greater effectiveness in the "nonprofit" sector. (Also, true.)

This kind of motivation, however, does not always speak to a personal benefit for front-line employees. As anxious as employees are for the company to succeed, the success of their employer does not always get them out of bed in the morning or put a skip in their step.

No, World-class customer relations brings fun to the workplace, and fun retains and motivates employees. Fun is infectious. Fun drags customers in and sets a continuing expectation for future behavior.

Sid ran a full-service gas station when he was younger. He organized competitions to see if workers could check the oil, clean the windows of the car and check the tire pressure before a fellow gas station worker could pump 10 gallons in the tank, for example.

The customers were aware of the ongoing competitions and would select this station for the entertainment value.

A useful way for a manager to diagnose the morale of her organization is to ask every employee at each encounter, "Are you having fun?" If the answer is yes, follow-up questions are rarely needed. Happy employees are more productive and receive higher ratings and better evaluations for job performance.

Customer service springs from optimism, respect for others, and high expectations. Workplaces, where fun is an organizing principle, provide outstanding customer relations. Grim workplaces rarely excite customers.

It does not matter whether the organization is a free clinic in an urban center, a fortune 500 organization, a school, or a tire shop. A climate that is fun and optimistic creates greater productivity and higher customer and job satisfaction.

This book will take fun seriously.

It is organized into three parts:

> **- On a practical level, how do front-line**

people provide good customer service?

- How do managers organize groups so that outstanding customer service happens?

- What are the organizing psychological principles that support world-class customer service?

World-class customer relations are intrinsic to the quality of the product or service. A management-consultant colleague, Larry Robinson, was a guest at a Ritz Carlton Hotel. He checked out of his room and worked at his computer quietly in the lobby while he waited for the hotel limo to take him to the airport.

The hotel must have announced the arrival of the limo but deep in thought Larry didn't hear the announcement. He glanced out at the hotel entrance only to see the limo leaving. He stowed his computer, grabbed his bags, and jogged after the limo down the street knowing in his heart, he had lost his opportunity to catch his plane.

Larry was muttering on his way back to the hotel, when a hotel gardener asked, "What seems to be the problem, sir?"

Larry explained the problem. The gardener guided him back to the lobby where the gardener addressed the front desk clerk.

The gardener said, "Mr. Robinson is a guest at our hotel. He has missed his limousine. He needs to catch a plane. Please issue me $25".

The desk clerk expressed her regret that Larry had missed the plane. She immediately gave the gardener $25. The gardener walked Larry to the door. He hailed a cab. He helped Larry put his bags in the trunk, and gave Larry the $25. The gardener said, "Here is $25. You will need $20 to pay for the cab. The other $5 is yours to do with as you please. If the cab driver gives great service perhaps you would give it to him. Have a nice flight back, Mr. Robinson."

Many things happened in that encounter. First, Larry Robinson became a devoted Ritz Carlton customer, and not surprisingly – so have the dozens of others who have heard the story. These individuals now have their own stories of outstanding customer service to add to the well-established Ritz Carlton brand.

More importantly in that moment of extraordinary customer service, the gardener and the person at the front desk each had a bright shining moment. They may have smiled the rest of the day remembering how they helped Larry. These smiles led to more customer service, which led to happy customers which…

The Ritz Carlton is not an unusually high-paying institution. Yet it retains not only its customers but its employees.

Life should be filled with small acts of kindness. What, in life, is more fun than helping others, or bringing a smile to someone's face?

That is the heart of a world-class customer service program, and why the best reason to give great customer service is to have more fun.

How do you behave in an elevator lobby? Have you watched others as they walk up to call the elevator? They press the elevator button to go up. The button lights, alerting everyone that the elevator system has received the request. However, some press it again and sometimes again and again and again.

Some people come to a bank of elevators. They press the button then the one across the hall, then the one at the next bank of elevators. They look at their watches and press them all again.

It is as if the harried button-pusher believes there is a computer saying, in response, "That lady on the fourth floor is in a real rush. Send her our elevator extra quickly".

How else can the behavior be explained?

Questions:

1) What brings real joy in your life?

2) Does making other people happy restore you?

3) What's one example of bringing a smile to another person that sticks in your memory.

4) Can you recall a tense situation that was made easier with a laugh or an act of kindness?

Part 1

Chapter 1
Serving Others
Serves Oneself

Help yourself live longer by helping others

Did you ever watch the automotive duels between two cars poised to seize the "close-in" parking space near the mall that the Toyota was leaving? The drivers' eyes are steely and focused, their chins thrust out. Their gas petal feet are poised and twitching.

Have you seen the nice people leave their church, synagogue, or mosque after a prayerful pause only to enter their cars ready to torch a fellow parishioner who had the bad taste to try to get to the main road first?

How about, in the grocery line marked "10 items or less"? What goes through your mind when some cuts in that lane with 12 items? Are you counting impatiently the number of items in the person's cart in front of you? Are you hoping the cashier will catch the offending customer with twelve items, and send her packing, clearing you for an immediate landing?

What is going on?

Are we all just five minutes short of nirvana? Would torching anyone between us and the exit bring us to paradise?

Why the pressure. Why the rude haste?

Would your life change if a distant relative gave you $227,000,000? Really… a $227,000,000 tax-free gift. How would you handle people who delay you then? Would the following fantasy be a possibility?

The man in front of you has twelve items and is in the "10 items or less" lane.

"Hello. Sir, I see you have 12 items," you might say in a casual and supportive manner.

"Yes, I do."

"Do you need anything else? I would be very happy to hold your place in line while you search for any additional items you may need or would like," you might say. "Don't worry about the cashier, sir. If he treats us badly, I will simply buy the store and fire him. Take your time, sir. I have your back," you could wink conspiratorially.

Would it change you, if you just were given $227,000,000? Could it change you?

This impatience and hurry that is at the heart of our rudeness might change if time pressures were removed. Are you different on vacation?

Does the heightened pace and stress of life in this fast lane increase rudeness in our customers and perhaps in us?

Most of our customers, like most of us. do not wake up in the morning hoping to find ways to be rude or abrupt to those around us.

Many of us do wake up in a hurry, however. The pace of our lives has changed. The quaint forty-hour week once was a reality. People had evenings free and uninterrupted weekends. Some even rested on Sundays. In many states and municipalities, stores were closed on Sundays. It was a day of rest, not a day to catch up on the responsibilities we failed to accomplish in the other six days.

People reported that they had the time to pursue an activity called dinner at home with the family.

A study indicated that one factor held in common by winners of national merit scholarships was that they ate dinner at home around a table with their families, uninterrupted.

Imagine? This is noteworthy in the study because most children don't eat dinner at home with their families anymore!

Should we lament these changes in our society and the increase in haste and rudeness? or should we do something about it? What do we owe our customers and ourselves? What is the moral imperative for our behavior?

The most important reason to give quality customer service is that you, the person in contact with the customer, will have more fun and so will your customer. Fundamentally, it is about fun.

If we do, maybe we, and our customers will discover what is uniquely human in us.

When we serve others with optimism and dignity, our enjoyment goes up. Would you like to help someone today? Of course. Who wouldn't? Altruistic people live longer. They report more life satisfaction. More than once, a nasty, greedy person has "got the best" of one of your authors in some commercial dispute. It is not a difficult task if the person "serving the public" has no ethics. We always walk away after being "had" consoling ourselves by saying, "At least I am not him (or her)."

Strive to reduce stress.

Did you ever notice that when flight attendants give you preflight emergency directions, they tell you that "in the unlikely event in a drop in cabin pressure, you need to pull that little clear tube tight and put the mask on yourself first? ..."

Why?

Don't they like children? No, that's not it. The reason? You can't help others put on a mask when you are unconscious from lack of oxygen. Take care of yourself first. Quality customer

service occurs when you care about yourself. You can help yourself by satisfying an impulse to generosity.

Help yourself live longer, be happier, be more productive, and have more friends, by helping other people.

Some statistics:

75% of visits to doctor's offices are stress-related.

Last year $400,000,000,000 was spent on stress-related problems.

Those people, who are overly stressed or troubled, have a 50% increased

Chance of serious illness or injury over their less-stressed peers

during the ensuing 5 years.

64% of marriages end in divorce, much of that related to stress.

Stress takes a toll. Helping others; giving quality customer service lowers stress.

Questions:

1) Does the heightened pace and stress of life in this fast lane increase rudeness?

2) Are there adjustments we could make in our personal lives to make us more resilient and therefore more accommodating of our customers?

Chapter 2

The Problem

68% of customers quit doing business with a company, primarily because of perceived indifference or no contact.

Satisfying an impulse toward generosity is what many others regard as virtuous or heroic. People admire kind people. An act of kindness lowers our stress and puts a smile on our faces. It also increases profit. It causes positive word-of-mouth advertising to go up and increases repeat business.

Why do many believe that the quality of customer service is going down? A negative attitude affects customers and affects employees.

"How are you today", Sid asked, cheerfully.

"Don't even go there. It's going to rain, sleet, snow, or hail", the woman said.

What is going on here? Why are some people like that?

Sid likes to share this poem:

Remember Me

I am the fellow who enters the restaurant and patiently waits while the waitresses finish their conversations before taking my order.

I am the fellow who goes into the department store and waits patiently while the clerks finish their "chit-chat".

I am the guy who drives into the service station, who never blows my horn and waits while the attendant takes his time.

You might say I am the good guy, but do you know who else I am? I am the guy who never comes back.

No one murders businesses; they just commit suicide on the backs of their disinterested employees.

Poor service has changed the syntax of our conversations.

"Hi," Fran says on the telephone.

"Yes," comes the faceless reply. (Since when is "yes" a reply to "Hi?") The person on the other end doesn't want to take the time to greet me and ask me what I want. She compacts it all into one word, inappropriately placed.)

"Is Diane in?" Fran continues.

"Just a minute", the voice replies. (Since when is "just a minute" a reply to "Is Diane in?") The response of this receptionist is common. But it is contemptuous of the language and Fran.

29

At the hotel, Sid greets the receptionist, "Hi".

"Reservations," the clerk asks. ("Reservations?" You bet! I have reservations about someone who won't answer a greeting with a greeting," Sid thinks.)

"Yes, my name is Sid Hulbert".

"We don't have you." ("You bet you don't 'have me'. I'll never come here again.")

Some people either don't know or they don't care how they come across.

"How do you want to be treated?" Sid asks this question at 200 seminars across the nation each year. The answers don't vary by 5 percent:

"I want to be addressed promptly".

"I want to be treated with respect."

"I would like to be greeted with a smile."

"I would like people to give me their undivided attention."

"I would like people to treat me in a friendly way."

One time in Jamestown, New York a woman in one of Sid's audiences replied that she "would like to be treated like a queen."

A man in the audience hollered out, "Hell, I just would like to be treated."

Treating people well is not a mystery. Yet, managers don't seem to "Get it".

Sid frequented a particular store in his hometown. They sold a product he liked at a price he thought was reasonable. The store was in a convenient location.

Yet, the people in the store didn't treat the customers well.

Sid always walked out with his product feeling he has been mistreated. It wasn't that they were nasty. They just were not nice. The people stocking the shelves did not take time to say hello or even acknowledge Sid if he said hello. The cashier did not greet him and she did not even seem to notice him when she gave him change. There was no "Have a nice day" or Take care"

She always seemed to be engaged in a conversation with the cashier next to her and was certainly not focused on Sid, a guest in her store. The store was dirty. The displays were not thoughtful, or well lit.

As a kindness, Sid approached the manager. Sid asked if he could have a moment with the man.

The manager sighed, and looked at his watch, impatient that a customer would interrupt his day. Sid could see firsthand where some of the problems originated. Don't you? What was the manager communicating when he glanced impatiently at his watch?

Do people treat you this way, too?

Sid explained to the man that there was a particular product that he liked in the store, that the store was convenient, and that the price was right but "the customer service was just not up to par".

"And?" The manager challenged Sid as if to say, "And your point is?"

"It is just that I am a customer. I have been a customer here for years. I am thinking of not coming back because your customer service is so bad," Sid replied.

"Is that it?" the manager paused again glancing at his watch. "That's where you are wrong. These people have all been trained in customer service and they are as good as you can get these days. The new employees we hire are not like our generation."

The manager's behavior was fairly typical of a certain kind of manager. They would rather blame poor customer relations on their employees' character or their customers, than on their own management skills.

For this man, the quality of the employees will always be bad. Sid was still unhappy and called the corporate office. He asked to speak to the customer relations person.

He explained that he was a long-time customer who regularly went to the store in his community to buy a particular product; that the price was fine; that the location was fine; but he was thinking of stopping his business with the store because the customer service was not up to snuff.

The corporate executive replied, "That's not true. I trained them myself."

Sid explained that he was a customer service trainer and that he felt he might be able to help. The man declined.

Sid asked, in a moment of inspiration, whether he could share a story with the man from the corporate office. "If at the end of this story you have not come to agree with me, I won't trouble you anymore today."

34

"Just move it along," the manager replied, probably looking at his watch, as well. Sid couldn't tell that on the phone, but he just knew that it was true.

"Imagine", Sid began, "that I have come to visit you at your house. We are having a drink standing in front of the fireplace; a dog enters the room, walks up alongside us, and craps on the white carpet. In this story, you have two choices. The first choice is that you can say, 'Who is that dog. I have never seen it before in my life. What is that _dog_ doing in my house?'"

"The second choice is you can say, 'That dog that crapped on the white rug is mine. I trained him myself.'"

Sid paused. The man sighed and said, "Is that it?"

"Well, yes," Sid said. "The people who work in that store are 'crapping' all over me."

"Maybe, that it is the way you tell it," The man replied. "I've got to get going now."

Sid does not shop at that store anymore. The store is continuing to go downhill. A new store, with a similar product line, has opened up in the town, sensing the opportunity. In time, the store with poor customer service will close. The employees will be laid off and when they close, the manager will be quoted in the local paper as stating that the reason the store closed was a declining economy in the region. Of course, all the former customers will know why it closed.

Employees who have worked at that store for decades may lose their pension, and investors will lose their investment. The local economy will be disrupted, and many families will suffer, in untold ways. But, the man from corporate "trained them himself".

It is the little things that crash customer service.

The things that bring companies down are tiny but accumulate over time.

Imagine you have entered a restaurant and have

waited eight or nine minutes to be attended to. No one has poured water or brought you a menu. Eight or nine minutes is not a very long time, but most of us find it to be an eternity when waiting to be served. So, it has been eight or nine minutes and the servers are talking earnestly in the corner while you quietly boil at your table.

Are there reasons for this apparent rude behavior on the part of the servers? There are always reasons. "It's not my table." Or, "Hilda's in the back, picking up a spill." Or, "It's only one more minute until the next shift comes in; We should not start to serve these people before the new shift arrives."

These may appear reasonable to the servers chatting in the wings, but they are not communicated to the customer and if they were, they would seem unreasonable.

There are always reasons for inattention or indifference to customers, but 68% of customers quit doing business with a company, primarily because of perceived indifference or no contact.

Phone customers report annoyance if the phone

rings three or more times before they are attended to.

Has any customer ever praised the dreaded phone menus, "Press two if you would like to…." Yet, look how those proliferate. Don't we know better?

It is always the little things.

Questions:

1) Has indifference toward you ever caused you to bring your business elsewhere?

2) Do you think it is fair to say hate is not the opposite of caring; indifference is?

3) Do you think periodic training about customer service might rekindle the desire to serve?

Chapter 3

The Little Things

How do you hug a porcupine?

The **STEPS** program represents a series of basic reminders for "front line" employees. (The people who deal directly with customers to improve customer relations.) Too often the things that make the difference in customer service are small. Yet the consistent application of these principles makes a huge difference, to you personally and the success of your business.

The **STEPS** program reviews choices that individual employees make in approaching their customers. Sid has been working with front-line customer service representatives and the managers of these critical people for 40 years. It's simple: when organizations focus on these very simple principles, customer service improves and profits go up. In the non-profit sector, customer loyalty has increased, and in both sectors, employee morale has improved.

What does the acronym S.T.E.P.S stand for?

S---Smile

T---Tone of voice

E---Expression/Facial

P---Posture or body language

S---Start putting into others what you want back

Chapter 4

S-Smile

First, take control of your attitude

Sid often asks his audiences, "How many of you want to have more fun?"

Not surprisingly, most people raise their hands to say they would like to have more fun. He then asks, "How many of you would like to have your customers treat you better?" Again, most people raise their hands. And then, "How many of you would like to have your fellow employees treat you better?"

The answers are all obvious. Most of us want to be with people who have a great attitude. Most of us would like to surround ourselves with our friends and families who are always ready for fun.

Most of us will settle for less, however. "Oh, her or him, sure, I would like to have a husband or wife with a better attitude but we have been married for 26 years."

"Them kids? They don't have a great attitude either, but what are you going to do? We made them."

We should be more demanding about peoples' attitudes, and that means we have to first take control of our own. Our positive attitude is the best way to influence others to have a positive attitude. What other tool do we have to help others to lighten up?

Our attitude is a choice. The choice we make when we choose our attitude each day consistently influences the attitudes of everyone around us.

The world-famous Seattle Pike Fish Market, retail outlet, has organized itself around four critical principles for success, one of which is, "Choose Your Attitude."

We can, and do, choose our attitude. Way too often, that choice is to our detriment.

Fran has been a regular volunteer at Camp Good Days and Special Times, a camp for challenged people in Penn Yan, New York. The camp supports childhood cancer victims, children of adults with cancer, the brothers and sisters of children with cancer, childhood AIDS victims, children whose families have AIDS, childhood victims of abuse, children whose families have been affected by AIDS, and ...You get the idea.

Although Fran has volunteered in many of the programs that the camp offers, he has primarily been associated with the childhood cancer camp. "It must be so sad," people often say to Fran when they hear of his volunteer work.

Of course.... it is not.

Children with cancer generally have learned that they can choose their attitude. We are not sure how, but they almost all seem to choose a great attitude. We all have a limited number of days on the planet. We can spend them as miserable, unhappy, grumpy people dragging everyone around us down and having an exquisitely miserable time or we can add to the planet's capacity for mirth.

Generally, at Camp Good Days, partially inspired by the generalized insanity of the staff and volunteers, the kids with cancer are laughing and having a good time.

If these children can and do choose optimism over pessimism, and smiles over frowns; what is our responsibility for our choices, those of us who are not being challenged with cancer? (At least, we hope you are not affected by cancer.)

We are faced with the choice, each day. How we will elevate others. A poor choice will impact us most directly but also everyone else we encounter. A string of poor choices will lead directly to a miserable day.

Sid often laughs about his first trip across Wyoming. It was, he remembers, a very long state. He remembers three things about that very long drive:

Grass. Antelopes

And a billboard which read, "Eat more lamb.

A thousand coyotes can't be wrong."

Partly because Wyoming is so long, that billboard played over and over again in Sid's mind. He even drove back to see if there was any fine print on the billboard. There was not. "Eat more lamb. A thousand coyotes can't be wrong." That was it. There it was. The point of the billboard was to urge people to eat more lamb, using coyotes as connoisseurs about the taste of those rangy animals. But Wyoming was long, so Sid kept thinking about it (and chuckling).

Sid, to his credit, chuckles a lot.

Don't miss what is in front of your nose. It's obvious. It's simple. But it will make all the difference on whether a business succeeds or fails. It will make the difference as to whether employees have fun on the job or dread going to work. It will make the difference as to whether your life is generally fun, or not.

If front-line employees should smile, managers should lead by example.

Don't smile all the time. (They will take you away and lock you up.) But do smile every time you make contact with another person.

The Sprint Call Center instituted a program to brighten the attitude of its employees. A supervisor was quoted as saying that she could hear the employees' smiles on the phone.

Do you think you can hear a smile on the phone? Of course, you can. A smile triggers a waterfall of physiological and psychological events. Physiologists have said that a smile can be very helpful. A smile accelerates the flow of blood and increases the oxygen to the brain. Smiles release endorphins that stimulate hundreds of other chemicals which generally improve our health.

Cancer patients thought to be terminal live longer if they laugh more. Some hospitals have installed humor rooms for cancer patients. Studies have shown that if the cancer patients laugh for two hours each day the patients both live longer and report higher satisfaction with the life they have to live.

We don't know about you, but we would happily spend a few hours in a humor room to extend our lives and remain healthier.

One time when Sid was explaining this to a group a man in the audience familiar with the research said, "Yes, but that humor room only works for a certain percentage of cancer victims."

I see... let's not endure the torment of laughter because enduring laughter might not extend every one of our lives. It would only work for most of us.

Would you volunteer for the humor room if there was only an 80% chance of it extending your life and making you healthier? Would you volunteer for the humor room if there was only a 15% chance?

We would volunteer if there was no chance. We might even volunteer if it slightly shortened our lives. Would you rather live 10 years smiling or 12 years frowning?

Sid is often asked, "Do you want me to smile even if I don't feel like it?", or "Do you want me to smile, even if it's insincere?"

Psychologists often puzzle over whether belief causes behavior or behavior causes belief. Does the smile happen because you are happy, or can you become happy by smiling a lot?

Do religious people pray a lot or if you pray a lot will you become more of a believer? Do people who exercise a lot get that way because they believe in the benefits of exercise or does committing that much time to exercise change how they feel about exercise?

There is pretty good evidence that, if you change the behavior, the psychology behind the behavior will also shift. A smiling person soon becomes happier. She discovers reasons to smile if she smiles more frequently.

Sid tells the story about arriving at the garage to pick up his car. It was supposed to be ready at 2:00 PM. He arrived at 2:15 PM only to discover that no one had yet looked at his car. Sid spoke to the manager.

"This is a problem for me. I have a very busy afternoon. The reason that I set up the appointment was that I did not have the time to wait while you repaired the car. I'm not angry, but I must tell you that I will take the car somewhere else if you cannot fix it right away."

"I will have the next available mechanic work on your car, as soon as he is free," the manager said.

Moments later a grumbling and irritated mechanic stumbled into the room, muttering, "OK, I am supposed to fix your damned car."

Sid took one look at that mechanic and said to the manager, "I would rather wait."

The manager looked puzzled. "Aren't you the guy

who was in such a hurry?"

Sid saw the manager's consternation.   He felt compelled to reply.

"Do you often do well on a delicate task when you are having a good day? Do things get worse when you are having a bad day? This guy is not in a mood that will heal my car."

He was right, of course. Stress hampers patience, manual   dexterity,   and   even   our   -problem-solving processes.

In a psychological experiment, patients were asked to choose between two physicians. The two "physicians" were actors playing the role of "doctor". One played the part of a senior, exceptionally skilled surgeon, with a bad attitude. The other played a "green" medical resident with little experience but a pleasant attitude. When asked which surgeon they would prefer to do their operation, the patients, almost universally, selected the medical student with little experience, but a great attitude.

As customers of even highly technical services, we prefer to be 'served" by people with a great attitude.

When Sid's father was scheduled for sensitive cardiac surgery, his family doctor recommended a highly competent doctor who happened to be pessimistic and grumpy. After meeting with the surgeon, Sid and his family decided to turn down that doctor and went instead to a hospital three hours away, where they found a doctor who was both competent and cheerful.

When Sid was waiting for his father to come out of that surgery, in a busy Houston hospital, he was seated in a position to watch the surgeons walk down the hall to the waiting room. Some of the surgeons would be smiling. Some would not. As a family member of someone in surgery, he was praying for a smiling surgeon. By the time Sid's father came out of surgery, it was late afternoon. Since six o'clock in the morning, the surgeons had been on their feet, often in a stressful, life or death situation.

As they broke through the double doors at the end of the corridor, many of the doctor's faces were strained and weary. Most of them, certainly the kind ones, remembered where they were going, and who they were going to see, partway down the corridor. They applied a smile and strode up to the patient's family, confidently. A smile is a way that we display confidence, competence, and optimism.

Weary as they were, those brave men and women, adjusted their attitude to meet the needs of their patients' families. The smile on the surgeon's face said all that needed to be said. Everything he said about the operation after that was merely a bonus. That smile was the key that opened the lock for the family. It was all they needed to "hear".

Sid was hired once to help a restaurant deal with its customer service. Sid watched the system already in place for a short time and approached the owner. Sid said, "The restaurant does a pretty good job with customer service all except for Mary. That woman is the meanest woman I have ever met."

"Oh, Mary, once you get to know her, you'll love her," the owner said, reassuring Sid.

"You like her, don't you?" Sid asked the owner. "You would like to see her continue to get paychecks and do well personally?"

"Sure, she's great!" the owner said.

"You'd be wise to pay her to stay home, then. That way she would be happy, and well paid, and your customer service would improve dramatically," Sid added.

"Oh, you just need to get close to her," the owner stated.

"How do you hug a porcupine?" Sid asked. This woman ought smile more and be more happily interactive with her customers.

Smiling triggers an attitude adjustment and sends a message about attitude, about the "smiler" to the customer, which is critical.

Some of the things Sid is asked to do, as a consultant, are a bit unusual.   In one of the most unusual jobs, Sid was hired by a rapidly growing company that needed to open a new division. They asked Sid to help them hire a new cohort of employees based on the applicant's potential to give world-class customer service.

Sid was placed in an office and interviews were scheduled. Sid asked each applicant a series of questions. One was, "Do you smile a lot?"

One particularly sour-looking man looked grimly straight at Sid and said, in response to that question, "I am known as a smiler."

"Perhaps you better tell your face," Sid thought to himself. Every single applicant had told him that they smile all the time. Almost no one smiled while they told him.

There were few smiles in the rest of the interview with that sour-faced man nor with most of the other people interviewed. Have any of the readers of this book been around too many smiling people today?Have people's smiles been just too annoying to you today? Are you typically surrounded by too many happy people?

We notice smiles because they are not that common. People who are smiling much of the time are memorable because they are rare.

Sid gained two insights from that experience interviewing for "smilers":

(1) Almost everyone thinks they smile all the time and

(2) Very few people smile all the time.

Most of the people reading this book believe they are very generous with their smiles. But the reader should ask him or herself whether their friends and family smile most of the time. The simple probability is that the reader, like the people Sid interviewed, probably doesn't smile as much as (s)he thinks (s)he does.

Should you smile even when you don't feel like it? Absolutely! We have a choice. We can smile and become one of those pleasant people that everyone enjoys being with ... or not. We can smile and become healthier and live longer... or not. We can live a life full of more happiness and fun by choosing to smile and be cheerful... or we can choose to be more miserable. As in most changes, it won't happen if we don't work at it.

Attitude, happiness and smiling are a choice. It is a choice critical to our health, the happiness of our family and friends, and our business success. Grumpy people are not viewed as people who give good customer service. They are not seen as competent, they get lower employee evaluations, and they are less productive. Further, their lives are shorter.

Questions:

1) Can we choose our attitude?

2) Do you know anyone who smiles a lot?

3) Is it fun to be around them?

4) Who would you choose as a surgeon?

Merely a competent surgeon, or one with a happy

and optimistic demeanor.

Chapter 5

T-Tone of Voice

If we can't even be sure about how we look, what are the chances we can understand the impact of our tone of voice?

The second step in Sid's STEPS program for front-line customer service representatives is *tone of voice.*

People establish their first impression of you in seven seconds. When people first meet you in those first seven seconds, they don't hear "what" you say. They hear how you say it. Research on job interviews indicates that the hiring decision is often made in the first few minutes.

The next time you are with a dog try this: Say, "Come here you nasty animal. I am going to beat you within an inch of your life." But, do it with a cooing, loving, warm tone. The dog will come immediately to your side, tail wagging, eagerly anticipating the encounter.

At a later point, call the dog, using these words, "Come here you, sweetheart. Come to papa (or mama). Come here, you darling." Only, this time, do it through clenched teeth. Use a mean tone. Be nasty. The dog will probably slink away.

Our tone probably communicates more than our words. A couple in that fresh bloom of new love teaches all of us how people long to be treated. One of them caresses the face of the other, looks deeply into the other's eyes, and murmurs softly, "I love you."

Years later that moment of affirmation is reduced to a passing and off-handed, "Love ya." The reply is too often something that sounds like, "UNGHH."

What does that mean, "UNGHH", a muttered utterance with no form or substance?

We wonder whether anybody reading this has had someone tell them that they love them, too many times today. Did they do it too sincerely? Did they look into your eyes too deeply? Were their soft tender caresses too intrusive in your life today?

You see, sometimes, we keep the words of support and caring, but we lose the tone of voice and the facial expression. The substance of the interaction disappears. Then people begin to ask, "What's wrong with this relationship?"

In romance, tone of voice is often the first casualty. Its loss will precipitate other losses.

Focusing on the tone of voice that we use with customers will do a great deal toward resolving conflicts and developing customer relationships.

One teenager attended one of Sid's seminars. When Sid was discussing the tone of voice, she turned to her mother and said, "So that's what you meant about me having a bad attitude." As a school superintendent for almost 30 years, Fran believes that if adolescents could follow these STEPS, parental problems with teenagers would be reduced by 50 percent.

We often see others more clearly
than we see ourselves.

For example, studies have shown that men generally see themselves as less muscular and less athletic than the women around them do. Women see themselves as fatter than the men around them do.

When people are asked to rate their appearance on a ten-point scale, 10 being gorgeous, and 1 being difficult to look at, the self-rating will often be quite apart from reality. Rarely does the self-rating match the ratings given by a group of people who do not know the person. If these independent raters rate them on the same ten-point scale, the views of the independent raters will be quite consistent with one another, but markedly different from the person rating their own appearance.

Some people will rate their own appearance higher than the independent evaluators and some lower. But few will be on the money.

Yet people see themselves in the mirror and photographs more frequently than they see almost anyone else.

How could this be? Freud has been discredited by many modern psychologists but his concept of "defense mechanisms" remains an anchor for modern psychology. This concept is critical to understanding human behavior.

When we are threatened physically, we rally to defend our physical beings. This is where the famous "fight or flight" syndrome comes into play. This instinct has saved billions of lives over millennia. It is a helpful tool.

Faced with a charging lion, we choose whether to fight the lion or flee, thus "fight or flight." Many factors go into that quick decision. Are we armed? Is the lion physically impaired? Are we on a Harley Davidson?

Yet the threats to us are not always physical. If someone looks you straight in your eyes and says "You stole the money off that table" and you see that they are serious, how would you feel? What would you do?

Freud would say we would react from a menu of choices that we have used since childhood designed to protect our self-concept (ego).

We might deny the accusation. "I did not." We might project it back on the accuser, placing the blame on the accuser. "No, you stole the gold." We might rationalize why a person might steal the gold to help the poor. We would choose from a menu of defenses we had been rehearsing since childhood.

The point is we instinctively protect our ego from external assaults just as automatically as we defend our bodies against potential physical assaults.

So, when we hear true but even mildly negative information about ourselves, most of us cannot easily allow that negative information to penetrate our defenses. Our immediate instinct is to hurl an ego defense.

Yet without kind and gentle feedback from trusted friends, most of us don't have any idea how we come across to others. If we can't even be sure about how we look, what are the chances we can understand the impact of our tone of voice?

Acquiring and maintaining a pleasant and warm tone of voice requires effort and feedback from others. We need to mine those critiques for the gold that lies within. We need to assess how we come across and craft a persona that works for us, our family and friends, and our business.

Questions

1) Can you remember a harsh teacher with a biting tone of voice?? How did that feel?

2) Did the teacher change how you felt about school?
Or even the way you saw yourself?

Chapter 6
E- Expression/Facial

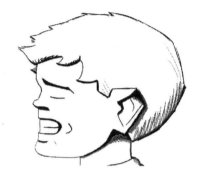

It is amazing that by manipulating facial expressions, some people can even manipulate the amount of stress their body feels, enough to fool a sophisticated test, like the polygraph."

This is very important. As you read the book, take a minute to find your happy and excited expression. Apply it to your face. Now try to say, with the happy and excited expression on your face, "You piss me off."

Or... "You make me mad." Or... "You are fired." As you can see, it is not easy to do and it never comes across as authentic, when you say these things with a smile.

Fran sometimes looks at the audience when Sid presents. Sid has a magical face. He takes more risks with his facial expressions than any other person Fran

65

ever saw.

So, Sid is in the middle of one of his colorful stories.

His eyebrows are raised high. His eyes are wide, and, his mouth is contorted to one side. Guess what Fran sees in the face of the people sitting in the audience... You got it! Their eyebrows are raised. Their eyes are wide and their mouth is contorted to one side.

People are natural mimics. That is how infants learn to talk and walk. Because we often learn from imitation, when you have a pleasant expression on your face, your customers will tend to imitate you and do the same. How you respond will influence how your customers respond.

Imitating the other person's facial expression is the first thing we all learn as infants. We never completely unlearn it. Make a funny face while telling a story and watch the listener(s) do the same.

There are two lessons in this observation about facial expressions.

Facial expressions do affect our customers.

Take a risk with your face. Be expressive, particularly about empathy, support, caring, and optimism.

One time Sid was flying home from a seminar when he opened a conversation with the woman sitting next to him.

She indicated that she was just returning from a seminar. Sid asked what kind of seminar.

"It was a seminar about administering polygraph tests," she answered.

"Why do you need to know how to administer lie detector tests?" Sid asked.

"I am a State Trooper," she stated.

Sid had to admit his surprise, but asked, "I've heard that people can trick a lie detector test merely by changing the expression on their face."

"Yes," the trooper said, observing Sid closely, "it takes a lot of work Most people can't do that, but I suspect you could."

Lie detector tests use multiple physiological measures to identify stress. Most people being observed while telling a lie will have increased stress. It will show up immediately in increased perspiration, increased pulse, and increased blood pressure. Multiple needles will jump. It is amazing that by manipulating facial expressions some people can even manipulate the amount of stress their body feels enough to fool a sophisticated test, like the polygraph.

I wonder if anyone who will ever read this book will indicate that they have just the right amount of stress, or will they all feel as virtually everyone does in Sid's seminars that they have too much stress?

The behavior of people at seminars is an indicator of their stress levels. People raise their hands timidly in response to a question, for fear of providing a wrong answer. They stand in the back of the room, in hopes of not being noticed. We all bear far too much stress.

The good news is that by changing our facial expressions we can minimize the impact of that stress on our bodies.

The best reason to give good customer service is that it improves our lives. A pleasant, warm, engaging facial expression impacts our customers the same way that the smile on the face of the surgeon impacts the families in the waiting room. And, it lowers our stress.

Our faces can shout about our empathy to the customer. We can convey strength or fear. I hope, if we ever meet, my face says, "I am so happy to meet you." It is what my voice will say, but if my face is saying something else, what I say will not be heard.

Below is a list of emotions, try to convey these emotions just with your facial expressions. Notice the subtle differences.

- You are welcome.

- Thank you.

- Please tell me what's on your mind.

- I want to help.

Wouldn't it be wonderful, if our attitude drove these expressions to appear frequently at work and home?

Chapter 7
P-Posture or Body Language

"People who like each other, while walking together, eventually will get their steps in the same rhythm. "

Body language gives us away. Tightly folded arms across one's chest, while tilted back in a chair, reveals skepticism.

"Oh, yeah?" screams the body of a person in that position.

It turns out we mostly read body language pretty easily. Most of us can't articulate exactly what we saw that let us know, but we understand the meaning of someone's posture. But let me give you a simple quiz.

A boy is shuffling toward you. His head is bent forward and turned slightly away. His shoulders are stooped. His arms are hanging loosely at his side. He does not walk directly toward you but just a foot or so to the side. He is looking at the ground. If there were a freshly broken lamp on the other side of the room, would you guess that the boy was feeling bad about the accident?

A young woman leans forward in her chair and looks directly into a young man's eyes at a restaurant, lips slightly parted. Her pupils are dilated. Her elbows are resting gently on the table cradling her chin. Would you guess that she had a romantic interest in the young man across the table?

A man leans forward in his chair. His arms are on the table in front of him. One elbow is resting on the table with that forearm slightly elevated. The knuckles of that hand appear almost like support for his head. His lips are resting gently on that knuckle and his eyes are cast softly downward. If you had just asked a tough question, would you think that he was taking that question pretty seriously and giving it some thought?

You observe a woman in a grocery store speaking to a young man. She is leaning forward. Her hand gesture is strong. Her thumb touches her index and middle finger. Her hand is jabbing at the air in front of the man. The hand keeps bobbing up and down rhythmically as she speaks. She stands comfortably erect. Her shoulders are square. If you were standing at some distance from her, would you guess that she is trying to make a particular point of emphasis?

If you answered yes to the four questions above, you are pretty typical. Most of us read body language pretty well. Sid argues that we read body language better than we listen. He may be right.

Our understanding of body language is probably instinctive. It certainly can be a tool that we can use to communicate with our customers.

In a tense moment with an angry customer, Sid's

body language seems unchanged from when he is relaxed.

Sid is quick to look people squarely in the eye, thrust out his right hand, and say "Hi. I am Sid Hurlbert. How may I help you?" Few of us are disciplined enough or mean enough to refuse to shake hands. Once you shake hands and look somebody in the eye, it is hard to be mean.

Sid tries to make every encounter personal, fun, and engaging. He makes his body do, around strangers, what it does around family and friends. Sid is alert to signs of resistance or discomfort, but he is quick to slap his hand on the back of someone he is talking to in a gesture that displays sympathy and friendship.

People-watching can be a great sport if you take it seriously. Fran worked at a college. People walk everywhere on a college campus. The buildings are often close together. So, all kinds of people walk together: students and students, students and faculty, faculty and faculty, faculty and deans, deans and students, presidents and students...

Here is an interesting observation. People, who like

each other, while walking together, eventually will get their steps in the same rhythm. Boyfriends and girlfriends holding hands put the right foot forward at the same time, and then the left. The lanky, long-limbed basketball player will stutter step to stay in sync with the short perky gymnast.

They don't do this on purpose. They just do it. Fran often sits by the window in the dining hall. If people don't get along, their steps will not be in sync.

He watches people walk together. He can usually tell the campus politics merely by watching them walk. People reveal themselves through their rhythms. People whose feet are badly out of step rarely agree. Rhythms are important.

The highest form
of flattery is imitation.

Our civilization depends on people imitating those people that they like and love. Why do babies imitate their parents? Why do we hope, or sometimes fear, students will imitate teachers? Intuitively we know someone likes us when they imitate us. We often know without noticing that someone likes us when they walk in sync.

We begin to notice that an acquaintance has become a friend, or a lover, or a confidant. We don't always know what in particular has signaled us to reveal that, but we know. The body language is communicating. We read it, we understand it, we make decisions and commitments based on it. Yet, it all happens beyond our understanding.

How can we use our knowledge about the importance of body language to help us work effectively with others? The answer, in part, is about rhythms and synchronicity.

A customer comes to make a complaint. We, of course, thrust out our hand. "Hi, I am Sid. How can I help you?" The customer stands, feet and shoulders wide, arms tightly folded, leaning forward. (This is a classic aggressive defensive posture,)

We have a choice. We can either assume an aggressive posture indicating we are up to the challenge he is about to make. Or we can initiate a softer and gentler body language, warm, expressive, and open, inviting our complainant to see our body language, and imitate it, and thereby change his fundamental psychological orientation.

The first option of pure imitation is pretty easy to do. Even those of us who don't have much formal knowledge about body language, can simply take the cues from our customers and move with them.

This approach may work. However, imitating aggressive body language may cause the customer to become even more aggressive. So, Sid takes a different approach. Sid begins with the outstretched hand, "Hi, I am Sid. How may I help you?"

This moves the person out of the most aggressive body language. Sid listens to the initial outburst, and then says, "Follow me." Sid walks to any other location in the store or office. The person follows Sid, usually to a counter or a desk.

Sid puts the counter between himself and the person. The person has to imitate Sid to get there. The customer follows Sid's rhythms. The body language has changed. Now Sid, "protected", by the counter, can safely indicate that he has empathy for the person's problem and is in touch with the person's emotions through his body language.

This method works better.

Actors study body language. They learn how to use their body deceptively to communicate to others powerful messages that they may, in fact, not be feeling. It takes years of practice for most people. Shortcuts here are hard to come by. But there is a method that may help someone in a customer service role get a head start.

This shortcut to learning how to use your body to communicate warmth, empathy, and caring is to "freeze-frame" moments when you are with people you like, doing things that you like to do. When you are in this moment, stop. Notice the way you are sitting, standing, and leaning. Learn how that feels. Reproduce it at times when you need to show other people that you are comfortable, and acting in their best interest.

Then roll it out in tense or not so tense situations so that others will see your body language and understand that you are a friend working on their behalf. At any rate, don't leave your body language to mere chance.

Sid went to a presentation about love and kindness by a very powerful scholar. Sid was thinking about how powerful the material was when he happened to notice that most of the audience was paying no attention, whatsoever, to the speaker. He wondered why until he noticed the grim countenance and hostile body language of the presenter.

What should the body language and tone of voice be of a person urging you to be more kind and loving? His brilliant words were lost due to his frowning face.

Sid does 200 seminars a year. He is often on the road and he has more experience than the average preacher speaking to crowds.

It is a funny thing to speak at seminars. Everywhere you go, there are certain commonalities. Preachers observe some of the same things. The back seats fill first. When you ask a question, rarely do people volunteer. When and if the hands do go up, they go up timidly. They raise briskly to shoulder height and then just as quickly retreat to the owner's lap.

What is that? Why are people like that? Why don't people stride down to the front seats and confidently raise their hands when a question is raised?

One time at a seminar at Cornell University, Sid confirmed his suspicions about why people act that way.

The audience was milling about in the entry foyer to the auditorium drinking the welcoming coffee and eating the bagels. The last few people were coming into the entry foyer. Some had just extinguished their cigarettes. The crowd had begun to enter the auditorium. A man was next to Sid as the audience funneled into that large room.

"Do you have to go to this damn thing, too?" The man asked. His face was contorted with barely contained anger.

Yeah," Sid said. "I suppose I do."

"I have so much to do, I could almost spit," the man sputtered. "I don't know why they are dragging me to this thing. This thing is probably just another huge waste of time."

"Probably so," Sid said.

"I am going to protest this one," the man replied. They probably are going to tell us to go sit down front, like they usually do."

"He is right again," Sid thought.

"This time I am going to protest. I am not only not going to sit upfront; I am not going to sit at all," the man sputtered.

"Me too," Sid said, "Where are you going to stand?"

"I am going to stand in the back," the man said. "The jerk that organized this thing won't get it, but I will feel better. I will feel like I made a statement."

"I agree with you," Sid said. "I am going to stand, too, all the way through this seminar. But I am going to do you one better. I am going to stand down front."

"Oh, don't do that. You'll get them mad," the man advised.

"I don't care. Something has to be done about this." Sid strode down to the front of the auditorium.

Sid stood leaning against the wall, his face glaring out at the audience.

The man standing in the back had a very worried expression and urgently gestured for Sid to join him in the back. Sid shook his head "no", defiantly. Sid held his ground at the side of the front of the auditorium.

The man in the back was worried.

Sid was making a fool of himself, he thought.

The man in the back regretted that he had suggested this protest. When Sid was introduced and took his place at the podium, the man slinked quietly to a seat.

After the presentation, the man approached Sid. "I'm sorry about all that stuff I said before you started. I needed this seminar more than I thought I did. Thanks for not embarrassing me by telling them what I did."

Sid smiled and hugged the big guy.

Body language makes a difference.

In the story above, Sid's body language, when standing against the wall in the front, was a mirror of the body language of the angry man. When he hugged him, he was warm and laughing. Body language helps.

We can smile with, tease, and cajole, even our difficult customers. The seminar and the interaction with Sid were probably even more meaningful for the reluctant attendee than for the rest

Questions:

**1) Can you tell by body language
that someone is angry, bored or happy?**

**2) When we fear someone is about to attack
us do you think it shows in our body language?**

Chapter 8

S- Start Putting Into People What you Want Back

> *"Our customers want to be treated respectfully. Wouldn't they like their encounters with you to be warm and comfortable?*

The last step in Sid's **S.T.E.P.S** program is to *start putting into people what you want back.*

Can you tell when someone is angry with you as they approach you? Is there something about their body language, facial expression, and demeanor that says that you are in for some trouble?

A lot of customer conflict comes from what we bring to the table. We can add stress to the encounter by our behavior. When we were just children most of us have had to deal with angry teachers, principals, and even, sadly angry parents. Encountering those powerful people when they are angry early in our lives, we had no effective way to develop a mature approach to deal with angry people.

Many of us and many of our customers have inappropriate reactions to stern, doubtful, or angry faces because our reactions to angry people were formed when we were too young to develop a reasonable response.

Here is a concrete example:

Sid loves to carry a tiny tape recorder. He loves to tape interactions with front-line people. He records the best and the worst and tries to learn from them. Sid bought a micro-cassette recorder from a well-known national chain when the recorders first came out. He was pleased that this tiny device would allow him to record these interactions, even more surreptitiously, than he could previously.

It was a new product line. The very first one he received didn't work. He returned it to the store, to a high school-aged employee, working alone at night.

How many of us hate to bring things back to the store where we bought them, even when we have the receipt and the product doesn't work? Most of us anticipate some level of conflict.

When Sid approached this young employee with his problem, the boy's face frowned. He folded his arms and asked, "How did it break?"

Sid knew immediately what the boy was asking, which was, "What stupid thing did you do, to break it?" Sid persevered, he explained that he simply took it out of the box, installed the batteries, and it did not work.

The boy played with the recorder. He also couldn't get it to work. Somewhat reluctantly, he gave Sid a new one. Sid went home, put in the batteries. And this one, too, failed to work.

How would you feel returning this second device to the same pimply-faced kid the next day? How would you feel asking, this time, for your money back and not simply

87

a replacement for this twice-broken device? As you entered the store, what's your facial expression? What is your body language? What is your demeanor?

The innocent high school student was watching, as the door flew open and a freight train bore upon him.

Let's pretend he was coached by Sid and knew what to do.

"I am annoyed," Sid might sputter. "This stupid cassette recorder…"

"Hi, I am David Tait," the boy might say, warmly thrusting his hand out to be shaken. How can I help you today?"

"Hi, I am Sid Hurlbert," Sid could mutter. His intent to be rude already thwarted. The context had just changed. This was no longer about a frustrating cassette recorder. It was now about two people just being introduced. The boy had begun to put into Sid what he wanted out.

Sid would then explain his problems with the cassette recorder and the history of this purchase. The boy (trained by Sid, remember) would say to Sid, "Follow me, sir."

(Mermer Blakeslee, author of the book, <u>In the Yikes! Zone,</u> a book about fear and negative emotions, talks about getting people out of fearful places by getting them to follow simple directions and moving them through simple rhythmical movements.)

Sid finds that asking customers to follow him takes the pressure out of the situation. He moves them to a second counter. Sid has now followed the young man's direction and is more compliant. The young clerk is now ready to solve the problem. The person in the customer service role has also had a few minutes to think while walking to the new counter.

When you put into other people what you want back, you can change other peoples' behavior.

Sid gets a lot of mail from members of his audiences where he presents. He got so much mail that the only practical solution for mail delivery was to open a post office box.

Sid did not like to go to that post office to pick up his mail. They were mean.

Sid had to go there to get his mail, but he didn't enjoy it.

Sid decided to put into them what he wanted back. He smiled. He used a lot of inviting facial expressions. He told stories. He engaged them personally. He expressed an interest in them. It soon became less of an "us-and-them" situation and more of a "we" situation, as they all began to laugh together.

One day Sid turned the combination lock on his mailbox. He opened the door. He put his hand in to retrieve his mail and as he did, a hand from behind the mailbox grabbed his. Sid nearly had heart failure.

When he retrieved his arm, he looked through the

opening, nothing could be seen but he heard peals of laughter coming from the area behind the mailboxes. He went to the customer service window and looked behind the mailboxes, where one person, who had originally been a particular old sourpuss, was laughing so hard that he was crying at the same time.

The breakthrough was complete. Sid had put into the post office employees what he wanted back, and he now looked forward to getting the mail. By controlling his own attitude and putting into them what he wanted back, Sid changed the way they behaved toward him. Can't we do this with our customers? Can't we take them on as projects, one at a time?

Once at the second counter, the high school-aged clerk can do what has to be done. Two of these recorders have failed. There was no alternative but to cheerfully return the money and express sincere regret. What else can you do? Let's do it stylishly.

Our customers want to be treated respectfully.

Wouldn't they like their encounters with you to be warm and comfortable? Couldn't this approach work for you?

Will this approach work for everyone?

No…Some won't try it.

There is an aspect of following this approach that makes one feel like a performer. "Do you mean that I have to be outgoing? Do you mean I have to greet my customer, shake hands, and introduce myself? Do you mean I have to smile at my customers and try to engage them?

Not if you want long days, miserable customers, and a failing business. If that is what you want, don't try these techniques. These techniques will have just the opposite effect.

Some people won't want to try this approach out of fear. They won't have the confidence. They may have no or low self-esteem. They may fear rejection. They may be concerned that they are too young, too old, too well dressed, or not dressed well enough. They may fear that they are too fat. They may be concerned about what will happen if the customer learns about their education or lack of it, their car, their house, or their neighborhood. "Suppose they meet my family?"

"I met your brother the other day," someone said.

"He is not my brother. He just says he is. Nope, not him, not that loud hairy guy."

A two-year-old could walk across a stage, buck naked peeing as he walked. He would smile, delighted to be watching the people watching him. He would not be self-conscious. He would remain confident, and at ease.

Life happened to us between when we were two years old, and today. Not all of it was good. A drop in confidence may have been one of the things we lost that we shouldn't have.

Kids, unaffected by our adult fears, can work us like a lion tamer works his lions.

All parents give kids the same instructions when they enter a store. "Don't touch anything. Don't ask for anything."

We watch them in the stores. The other day we watched a cute little four-year-old girl pick up toy after toy in the discount store. She begged. We were too far away to hear the father but we could see his lips say no. As she brought each item to his attention, she dropped a shoulder and got a sincere and pleading look on her face.

I was prepared to shove him out of the way and buy the toys for her myself.

She managed to put one of the toys in his hands and when he picked it up, she applied a very hopeful smile on her face. I was sure he would tumble this time. He put it in the cart. She won again. She rewarded him with a face-splitting smile.

Here is the critical question. Did that four-year-old girl go out to the car and read a book on how to handle rejection and how to get what she wants?

No.

We all start out being pretty good at this and get worse when we begin to believe the negative things that people tell us about ourselves.

Sid is an interesting case in point. He was a pretty good student at Penn Yan High School in New York. But college was not in his future.

College was simply not a part of his family's experience. No one had planned for the college tuition costs. His counselors and teachers did not urge him to go to college, despite his good grades. He didn't come from a college-oriented family. In those days that may have been a more important cause of college admissions than academic laurels.

When he finished high school, he worked and started businesses where his extraordinary ability to work well with customers became celebrated. In time, Sid was making presentations across the country. Large and small businesses including universities brought him to speak frequently. He lived in terror, however, of being asked

"What college did you go to?"

We all seem to have reasons to hide rather than shine. Sid is not going to change his educational background. He is running seminars 200 days a year. He does not have the time or the+ inclination to go back to school. There are things about all of us that cause us to retreat into ourselves instead of coming forward confidently.

Often these reasons are old, foolish ones, like Sid's concern about not having gone to college. Hell, now Sid trains college professors.

One time Sid was the second speaker on a program. The first speaker was handsome, slender, and well dressed. Sid is anything but slender. The first speaker's high level of education seeped out in his language.

Sid is plain-spoken. Sid watched the man on the stage and, for one of the first times in his life, he thought, 'I don't want to go on. I don't want to follow him."

There are days like that for all of us. Sid forced himself onto the stage. He reached out to shake hands with the first speaker as they passed each other walking across the stage. The speaker did not take the offered hand. Sid pulled back his arm, embarrassed, and kept going. He was sure everyone there saw that snub.

Sid didn't want to be there speaking after the snub. But he dug deep. He smiled. He put into his audience what he wanted back. He modulated his tone of voice and brought a warm empathic facial expression to his presentation. The guy who spoke first wanted to talk with Sid after he saw Sid's presentation. He asked Sid to share with him how he had connected so well to audiences.

The other speaker wanted to achieve what Sid had.

Sweet revenge.

Questions:

1) Do you think that we can change the attitude of some customers by putting into them what we want back?

2) What are the specific behaviors you would want from someone serving you if you were a customer?

Chapter 9

Confidence
is Crucial

We would all be more effective if we followed Sid's **S.T.E.P.S.** program. But we have to recapture the confidence we had in pre-school, we need to risk trying new methods.

Sid had an experience with an airline that put a fine point on this. The story is a common one, as it begins. An earlier airplane had skidded off the runway. Many flights to and from Chicago were canceled including Sid's. He, and a lot of other people, were stuck in San Antonio waiting to get to Chicago. Sid led with his optimism. He controlled his tone of voice and his facial expressions. He smiled at the airline representative.

He put into her what he wanted back. He teased her, played with her, and engaged her warmly. He explained that he was due to present the next day in Chicago, at a seminar for 240 people. There was no alternate date.

The airline representative began typing furiously searching for a ticket for Sid. She put together a flight that took two stops to get Sid to Kenosha, Wisconsin. Sid could rent a car from there and make it to Chicago on time.

Sid was pleased.

Sid asked the woman, "Were the flights that these other unhappy travelers needed already full?"

"No, they are practically empty," she replied.

"What will happen to these other people?" Sid inquired.

"I guess they will have to cool their heels," she

replied. "Sometimes people get what they deserve, especially when their attitude is poor. I don't owe these people anything. You, you're different."

The **S.T.E.P.S**. Sid shares with audiences across the United States are all pretty basic. Most of us can easily understand that if we consistently employ these S.T.E.P.S., we would be more effective with our customers.

Unfortunately, familiarity breeds comfort.

We find little personal risk in continuing to do what we have always done. There is, however, little chance that we will improve our relationships with others, by staying the same. Not changing brings no risk of embarrassment, but it ensures not improving over where we are now.

Most of us will be trapped in San Antonio, as "we deserve". Some of us will take some personal risks and be routed to Kenosha. From there, with initiative, we could drive to Chicago. Those of us who do change may get to where we want to be.

Questions:

1) Are you prepared to take a few small risks to improve your customer service?

2) If you become legendary in customer service, would the risks you took to get there be worth it?

Chapter 10

Celebrate People

"If we abuse the members of the team because of our blind commitment to the task, we will be locked in a downward spiral."

Earlier we talked about the power of habit. We can become captives of our habits. Sometimes that is a good thing. Bathing is a habit that works pretty well. Sid and Fran are pleased to report that each of us has a habit of bathing. It makes it easier when we get together with people who have noses.

Habit takes a funny hold on us. There was a report not long ago that men each shave their face the exact same way every time. Sid starts on the upper right on his face, works toward his chin, and …He tried to start on the left and nearly required a transfusion from the loss of blood that resulted from the razor nicks. The whole skillset of shaving is based on a series of sub-routines that are conducted in a particular sequence. Changing the order requires a complete reconstruction of the task.

Habit is not always a bad thing. Habit is why Major League Baseball players can hit the ball with some consistency. It is why good golfers have a pattern of success.

Wouldn't it be awful if every time we reached for a cup of coffee we had to solve the problem of how to take a sip?

Much of our life is spent in repetition. Our habits in the morning, from the moment we turn off the alarm clock until we arrive at work, are usually routine. Our habits help us to get through the day efficiently, even while half-awake.

Not all habits, however, are helpful – especially those that belittle other people.

Most of us are unaware of these habits unless other people bring them to our attention. Even then, we tend to reject them. ("My boss told me I am sometimes abrupt…that idiot, what does he know?") It is hard to hear this kind of criticism. We all think we are pretty good with people. If you look around you, however, you'll realize that someone who is truly gifted with people is unusual. Objectively, we cannot all be great with people. Probably, if you are like Sid and me, you could stand some improvements in this area. Who couldn't?

The habits we have that are not great in our dealings with people we probably did not select. Children are like sponges for new information and behaviors. As we get older, our ability to learn declines. (There is pretty good research, for example, that very few people can learn a foreign language without an accent after the age of 12.)

So, while we are being human sponges, powerful adults in our environment show us how to treat others, for example, when they are disappointed. Those role models are parents, teachers, scout leaders, coaches, principals, and others who dealt with us when we disappointed them.

So, Joyce who works with Sid and Fran comes into the office a little frazzled from difficult deadlines and complex tasks. Fran says to Joyce, "Did you get that letter out to Ralph?"

"Oh darn, I forgot." Joyce might reply, disappointed in herself.

The most important thing Fran will do that day will happen in the next millisecond. Sid likes to say that you feel 30,000 times faster than you act, and you act 30,000 times faster than you think.

Most of us are going to act before we think about it, based on a feeling of disappointment which will cause our blood pressure to rise. As a species, normally we approach this moment as a "ready, fire, aim" situation rather than a "ready, aim, fire" situation. Our behavior is so fast it feels like we don't have any control over it. Do you ever regret those moments when you fire from the lip?

What we do at that moment, is to play the old tapes from childhood. We might roll our eyes. We might shake our heads no. We might say, "tsk, tsk, tsk." We might explode in pointless rage.

There are, of course, better options.

Joyce is a remarkable person. In her heart, she wants Sid and Fran to succeed more than they do. She gets it right 95 percent of the time. Ninety–five percent got her pretty good grades in high school, college, and graduate school. Her accuracy and follow-through made her a successful teacher and school administrator.

What should the response to Joyce be? How could Fran respond, leaving her ego intact? How could Fran communicate to her about this, and let her know that she is a valued member of the team, a friend, and a person that he cares about? How about, "Pobody is nerfect."
Because nobody is perfect.

We should never let go of our task orientation. If the work is not important, perhaps we should be doing something else. It is not appropriate to abandon the commitment to the task.

But, if we abuse the members of the team because of our blind commitment to the task, we will be locked in a downward spiral. We need to look at our habits in dealing with people and to adopt new behaviors that celebrate the people in our lives.

Questions:

1) Are all habits good habits?

2) Was Twain right that habits cannot just be flung out the window?

3) Are all the behaviors we saw from the adults we observed in our youth worth continuing to follow?

Chapter 11

Handling Mistakes

> *"Pobody
> is nerfect."*

Mistakes are inevitable. Fran notes that he, like Joyce, has about a five percent error rate. About five percent of the time, no matter what he is doing, he will make a mistake. Five percent of the time when he leaves his driveway, he turns the wrong way. Five percent of the time when he goes to the grocery store, he brings home the wrong item or forgets something.

These mistakes cut across the big issues, too. Five percent of the time as a school superintendent, he screwed up a conversation with a taxpayer, a citizen, or a parent. Most of the time, these mistakes are not critical. When turning the wrong way coming out of the driveway, you turn around and come back. They are not very costly because, frankly, most of what Fran does, in life, is not a life-or-death decision.

Are any of us dramatically different from this? Some people have a two percent error rate or a three percent error rate. Even so, it is an error rate. Error is a constant. It may be impossible to remove it from any human system.

Yet, even though we all make mistakes, sometimes we handle another person who made a mistake, the way people handled us when we made mistakes as children. "How could you be so stupid?" Or, "Did you leave your brain at home today?" Or "Why don't you use your head for something other than a personalized hat rack?"

It may be fun to hurl these types of insults, but they surely do more harm than good.

Our brains are imperfect computers. It is easier to engineer a computer chip to make no errors than an organ with blood vessels, cholesterol, and a high degree of reliance on oxygen and micronutrients. Some error would be expected by the nature of the design of the organ called the brain. After all, even some of those computer chips sometimes make mistakes.

Can the brain be confused by not enough sleep or exercise? Or by an emotional uproar?

We do need to provide feedback for our employees that can help them see the gap between their performance and the company's goals. But the feedback should be designed to be respectful.

Why do we jump all over somebody who made a mistake? The mistake has already been made. There is often little the person can do to unmake some mistakes. The work should go into helping them not make the mistake in the first place by defining the task better and "dip-sticking" their performance early, on all the sub-tasks that lead to the eventual success or failure of their work on the larger mission.

When a person says, "I made a mistake", they, of course already know they made a mistake. That is often how you find out about it in the first place. Most people feel very badly about mistakes, especially the serious ones that hurt others. They don't generally profit from being berated.

Sid had a four-hour seminar at a company that had made attendance mandatory for a group of employees. The group was mostly present. Sid moved forward to the microphone. He smiled at the group in anticipation of launching his presentation. Just as he was about to begin, a woman charged into the back of the room. Sid observed her, still in her coat, carrying her briefcase. She looked at him and gave an exasperated sigh.

Not all of Sid's thoughts at this moment were happy ones. He thought "this is going to be a tough group." He thought "I am sorry she made it."

However, he spoke to her across the noisy room in a kindly voice, "We've not yet begun. Why don't you hang up your coat and get yourself a cup of coffee? I will begin in a few minutes." She glared at him still as if he were the one being rude and then, hung up her coat and got coffee.

Sid is a very effective presenter, and a lot of what

he shares touches people's hearts. Some of the points he makes will cause tears.

In an audience exclusively with men, when Sid touches on those points in his presentations, there will be a lot of throat clearing. Women feel more at ease crying.

The woman who arrived late got to such a point in his presentation, where he was talking about the need for parents to treat their children with dignity. She began to fall into shoulder shaking sobs.

When the presentation was over, she approached Sid as the other employees were exiting the room. She explained to Sid that earlier, that very morning her husband announced that he was leaving her. He was moving in with another woman. He was filing papers for a divorce. He provided her a date when he and the movers would come to pick up his stuff.

As her husband left the house their 11-year-old daughter looked her mother straight in the eye and said, "It's my fault, isn't mommy?"

"I dropped her off at school, trying to explain cheerfully, what I had experienced tearfully."

The woman threw her arms around Sid's shoulders. "Thank you so much," she said. "I needed this seminar more than I knew. Today I learned my husband of 15 years is divorcing me. My daughter thinks it is her fault. I was running late and feeling terrible. When I came into the room, I thought that you were going to attack me because I was late. Instead, you were nice to me, and what you said helped me very much."

We cannot know all that goes on behind the eyes of the person looking at us. Most of us have seen too many examples of how others have used an ill-considered reprimand, sarcasm, or even an "off-handed" gesture, to put people in their place. We need to find better alternatives than the examples that may have been provided to us.

Would we be better or nobler and more effective, if we respond instead with empathy, while still insisting that we all work to improve the system for our customers?

Questions:

1) Do you prefer to be corrected in public or in private?

2) Do you find it better when the person correcting your errors is quiet or loud?

3) Are you happier when the discussion after you make a mistake begins with, "We all value what you do here very much, and God knows we all make mistakes, but...?

Part Two

Chapter 12

An Introduction to Reframing

Reframing is also a simple idea. It takes initiative and practice to apply regularly. That is why Sid doesn't introduce it, except by example, in his introductory seminars. It only works if people use it with a twinkle in their eye. Sometimes it doesn't work at all. We can use it on ourselves and others, individually or in groups.

Much more often than we would like to admit our thinking gets stuck. Our response to others gets mired in a familiar rut. At these times, we too often see the world with blinders on. Let us provide you with an example.

Although there is some debate about the facts about the way European sailors saw the world before 1492, most of us understand that European sailboats stayed pretty close to the European continent. For some, there may have a fear of falling off the edge of a flat world. Others simply were afraid of the imagined size of the sea or afraid they would not find their way back.

It took Columbus' insight and his brave act of sailing to the "new" world to reframe our vision of the world. He made us see it as a continuous sphere.

Reframing is the act of suddenly putting the world in a new context. Once that happened, the behavior of European sailors was dramatically and permanently altered. That's an example of reframing.

We all hear the dictum," Think outside the box". One of the disciplines of thinking outside the box is to continuously reframe. People who fail to reframe miss opportunities because their vision is limited. The railroad ran into difficulty, not because of the airplane. They ran into difficulty because they didn't see their business as the "transportation business". The railroad execs thought they were in the "railroad business". Transportation incorporates all forms of travel which could include even air travel and air cargo.

If the railroad executives had seen their mission more broadly, Sid's next business trip might be booked on Flight 600 on the Santa Fe and Topeka airlines.

Sid reframes people, places, and events all the time. A waitress grumpily approached him once demanding, in a surly voice, "What do you want"?

His reply was, "I'll have a new waitress, please."

His reply reframed for that waitress the standard of customer service that some customers expected.

An old habit of the waitress was challenged with an unexpected reply. Her old habit was, "I am an order taker. I don't like doing this, but they pay me. I will do it, but I don't have to be happy about it." Sid's reply caused her to reframe her behavior. For her, it was the equivalent of Columbus discovering America.

As we will discover later in this section of the book, this act of reframing could not have been done effectively by someone whose demeanor was sarcastic or belittling. It needed to be done by someone who, like Sid, had a twinkle in his or her eye.

The waitress was startled at the reply from Sid. But she saw he was serious. Reluctantly, she left. Sid got another waitress. He teased and joked with the new server each morning during his week-long stay in that town.

He would sometimes begin the day by giving the new waitress a big tip. Only then did he explain he wanted her to see the tip first so she would know the kind of service he expected.

Toward the end of the week, the grumpy waitress asked Sid if she could try again. Her attitude and service were great. During the remaining days, she continued to serve Sid well. On Friday, the owner of the restaurant told Sid, "I am going to hate to see you leave."

But Sid could leave. His job was done.

We need to understand that change has enemies.

Sometimes it seems the whole world is aligned against change. Our defensiveness is one of the most prominent enemies of personal change. Defenses were a good thing for our species, historically. When our enemies were stalking us across the African Veldt, our defenses were what kept us alive.

Facing a physical threat, our automatic response was "fight or flight". Facing one small lion while armed with a sharp spear, we might fight. Facing a pack of lions, we might exercise our option for flight and run. Those responses, fight or flight, still help us in a complex and sometimes threatening contemporary environment. Who, reading this book, has not said, "I'm not paying for this! This is ridiculous. You have to take it back." Is this the contemporary instinct to fight?

Who, reading this book, has not hastened her pace back to her car upon hearing footsteps behind her? Is this the same instinct "wired-in" two million or more years ago for flight?

These are contemporary examples of fight or flight.

Defenses can be good. They protect us. +We have all kinds of new ways to defend ourselves in this era, equipped as we are with language. We use sarcasm and ridicule. We deny accusations.

We lie even to ourselves.   We counter-attack. We project our inadequacies and attitudes on others. We blame others for our faults. This is just a beginner's introduction to the sophisticated defenses we use in the 21st Century. Defenses are good, you see, except when they stop us from seeing ourselves clearly which can stop us from moving ahead.

As a species, we used to wield defenses to defend our lives. Now, we use them to defend our egos. Language made defending ourselves easier. Some would argue these "post language" defenses made that "ego defense" way too easy... to our detriment.

Earlier in the book, Sid asked the question, "Who doesn't give good customer service?" When he asks that question in a group, even in a large group, no hands go up.

We all think we give good customer service. It is easier for us to see when someone else does not give good customer service to us than it is when we fail. Our defenses don't let us see our behavior when we fail to provide the same support to others that we crave.

The person we all identify as giving lousy customer service probably also has great defenses. There are reasons for the poor customer server's behavior. (S)he can't change. (S)he is blind to his/her faults. His/her defenses make him/her blind.

"Are you kind?" we ask, rhetorically.

Are you? Earlier we used the image of Columbus discovering a new world. Soon after his discovery, mapmakers labeled the new world now known as North and South America as "Terra Incognita" (the unknown land). For each of us today, the "Terra Incognita" is too often, ourselves. Are you kind? Do you know?

Try this simple test of our self-knowledge. Are you good-looking? Do you know? Few of us do.

We see others more clearly than we see ourselves. We don't bring as much baggage to the appearance of others, especially if we don't know them. But, to ourselves, we bring steamer trunks of baggage.

Why don't we know how we look when everyone else apparently does?

Our ego defenses don't permit us to see ourselves. They are so powerful; they cloud our vision of ourselves.

If we are so blind that we can't even accurately see how we look, what other aspects of our lives do we not "see"? Could insight into our strengths improve our performance? Could insights into our weaknesses do the same? If we could see our assets and liabilities, would it help us be more effective?

The revered Scottish poet, Robert Burns, upon observing a beautifully coiffed woman seated ahead of him in church, with a louse crawling up her hair said, "Oh, would some power, the Giftic gie us, to see ourselves as others see us." Translated into contemporary English, it would read, "Oh, would you Lord give us the power to see ourselves as others see us!"

The woman was poised in the church pew, basking in her own presumed beauty, not realizing that there were bugs in her hair. Yet, Everyone else could see them. How could that be? Is it always thus?

Psychologists consistently report that peoples' self-rating of their job performance is generally higher than their bosses' rating of their performance. This will come as no surprise to anyone who has had to evaluate personnel.

These are all predictable problems that come from a well-developed set of ego defenses. That which kept us safe from lions, tigers, and bears (oh my!) interferes, in a highly competitive age, with our ability to assess how well we provide our customers with what they want.

Reframing has the potential to provide short intense sparks of insight.

Since the 1960's the psychological literature on

change has stated that three conditions have to be met for change to occur:

People and organizations have to have a clear sense of where they want to be. They have to, as Senge states, begin with the end in mind. (People have to have a clear picture of what world-class customer service would look like in their organization before they could make it happen.)

People and organizations have to understand where they are now, exactly. This is very hard to do. Defense mechanisms stop us from seeing our faults. (Remember, most people think that their customer service is great.)

People and organizations have to want to close the gap between where they want to be and where they are now. (At this point, coaching is often helpful.)

Frequent and objective monitoring can keep the changes in place and open new areas for exploration.

Seen from this perspective, change is not complicated. If all the above conditions are met, it is hard to stop people and organizations from changing. So, what's the problem? First, people don't see where they are. Second, they often don't have any idea of what a better approach might look like. If people don't see a problem, they can't move to fix it.

Why don't we just tell the "mean-spirited" waitress in the story that she has to engage in a kindlier way with her customers?

We'll tell her she is terrible the way she is; and, that her customers expect a more considerate approach.

"You are a real nasty waitress. Shape up or ship out", Sid could have told the mean waitress in the restaurant.

Now, there's a good idea!

Not so much.

This would work splendidly if people didn't have

those pesky ego defenses hardwired in. But they do. After two million years of success with these defenses, it is hard to throw them overboard. Mark Twain said, "Habit is habit, not to be flung out the window, but to be coaxed down the stairs one step at a time."

To confront people directly about their rudeness, their lack of consideration, or service inadequacies, is to attack them at a very fundamental level of their personality. The possibility of rejection of your helpful suggestions is very high. This strategy is unlikely to succeed, in most cases. We have all seen it work sometimes, but it fails far too frequently to turn to it all the time, as our primary method to resolve customer service problems.

Here is another approach that will fail as easily as the first. Let's provide a lecture to the waitress about good customer service. Let's show her why valuing our customers is important. This approach is designed to give the waitress a clear view of where she needs to go without, addressing the question of where she is now. She may say, indignantly, "Why is he raising these questions with me? Or, she may ask, "What has this got to do with the price of tea in China?"

Worse yet, let's haul in the whole staff to address the problems of one low-functioning employee. The whole group will get the lecture, hoping that the one bad apple gets the message. The "good" staff will know who you are trying to address and resent the mandatory lecture. The troubled staff member will still not see this as her problem.

Ask any teacher who is skilled at her craft, and she will tell you that teaching is not a group activity. Great teachers engage each student, one at a time, and pile up their successes, one student at a time.

If the reader has attended a seminar by Sid, she will know that other people were in the room when they attended his seminar, but Sid was engaging her alone. Sid is a great teacher.

We have all heard the expression, "When the student is ready, the teacher will come". How many lessons have we heard from our parents, teachers, and others that we were simply not ready to hear? We failed to learn, simply because we were not ready for it.

Were you one of the 90 percent of us who failed to get it when you were told "Don't run up debt?" Do any of us have poor finances because of a lack of information about the dangers of indebtedness?

Fran always marvels at the problems the public believes can be solved merely through education. Drug and alcohol education will surely stop the abuse of drugs and alcohol. Kids won't use them once they know the risks. No, drugs and alcohol won't recruit new kids. Or could it be that kids will discover it is fun to get stoned? And, sex education…don't get me started.

It is not that we should not provide information to children about the consequences of drug and alcohol use and abuse, and about sex. They should understand the consequences of their behavior. But warnings, relayed in groups, will not stop what men and women have been doing since Adam and Eve.

If we don't perceive a need for change, all the sage advice and lessons that are given to us, will simply not matter.

Reframing is simply a way in a singular moment to come "up sideways" on people about problems, not head-on. Coming at it head-on raises defenses. Coming up sideways, in a startling way, allows the message to sink in, sometimes.

Scott Shablak is an extraordinary teacher. When Fran taught with him in a middle school, in Onondaga County, in New York State, there was one particular student who had a problem no one else seemed able to fix.

"Pete" was a student at that school. There is one of these boys, like Pete, in every middle school. Maybe you remember the one in your middle school, growing up.

He traveled through the hallway as if he were a car. He made car noises as he moved, and frequently "upshifted" and "downshifted" using his hand on an imaginary shift knob while adjusting his vocalization.

Ask any middle school teacher, and they will identify which student, in his or her school does this, all the time.

130

These boys, (they are almost always boys) can be pretty geeky. They often use their "automobile selves" to keep other people away. The behavior isolates them, happily.

Many teachers had spoken to the boy about the "car" behavior urging him to stop it. They told him in a kindly manner indicating that this behavior was inappropriate. They told him that he would have an easier time making friends if he stopped doing it. Teachers spoke to his parents. The parents then spoke to Pete about the "problem". He wouldn't give it up.

Scott Shablak understood reframing. Scott and Fran taught in the same classroom.

"Watch this," Scott said, as he reached for a small spiral-bound assignment pad. He grabbed a pen and waited by the door to the room, anticipating the sound of our young "automotive boy", Pete. As we heard the sounds of the gearshift coming up the stairs and along the hall, Scott leaped out the door with a flourish. He held up an outstretched palm, in a gesture that said, "Halt!" Then Scott said dramatically, "Pull over to the curb".

Pete, the "Automotive boy" downshifted to a stop at the edge of the doorway with a startled look on his face. Scott was speaking to him using the very grammar and syntax of his behavior.

Scott dramatically flipped open the assignment pad. He licked the tip of the pencil and held it in position, poised over the pad. "License and registration?" Scott snarled.

The boy looked very uncomfortable and squirmed.

"No license? No registration?" Scott demanded.

The boy looked crestfallen. Scott began to scribble. He said aloud what he was writing, "Unregistered motor vehicle, and unlicensed driver not to mention speeding. These are very serious offenses."

The boy began to stammer as if attempting an explanation.

"I'll let you off easy this time, but if I see you

anywhere on this highway again, I will throw the book at you. I am going to impound the vehicle, and if it happens again I will put you in jail. Leave the car here for now. You can go on, but you are on foot from now on. If your parents want the car back, they can come and get it. But for now, it stays here. Got that?"

The boy sheepishly walked away. Curiously, he never "drove" again.

This was a straightforward case of reframing. Scott put the problem in a different context. He brought the boy's attention to the problem without raising his defenses. He attempted to resolve the problem symbolically. In this case, this symbolic resolution was the resolution. In other situations, reframing brings clear insight into the problem without truly resolving it. Recovery can sometimes require additional steps and support.

Reflecting on the rude waitress example from earlier in the book, the waitress was surly. She didn't know she was difficult. Her tone was, "What do you want, Mac?" That's not what Sid wanted. What he

133

wanted was "What can I do to help you this morning, dear?" Sid is pretty good with mornings, but none of us likes our morning to be jarring.

What he said was, "I'll have another waitress."

His request provided him with a different waitress, and as you will remember, from earlier in the book. The rude waitress got better.

The interesting part of this story was that Sid stayed in this town for a week, and the surly waitress came back after a few days asking if she could try it again. This time, she did it beautifully without flaw. You see, when she discovered how she was, she didn't need much help.

She already had an archetype of how she wanted to be. She knew what a good waitress was. She had just made the simple mistake of thinking she was one. Her defenses clouded her vision.

The change was then easy. Sid was able to come at her sideways in a startling way that let her gain new insights into her behavior by reframing the problem. Once she understood what she was doing wrong, she adjusted it. Very few people want to be bad at what they do.

Reframing is based on a set of principles in psychology best described by Perceptual Control Theory. For those of you who want to learn more about Perceptual Control Theory, one of the leading academic authors is a man by the name of William T. Powers. His major but somewhat stuffy book is <u>Making Sense of Behavior.</u> More readable presentations have been written by E. Perry Good. She wrote many accessible books. A good introduction is in a volume called <u>In Pursuit of Happiness</u>.

Perceptual control theory holds that people do not like an imbalance between the picture of where they want to be and where they are at the present.

Earlier psychologists described a similar imbalance as "cognitive dissonance". Some researchers have reported that many different varieties of neurosis spring from cognitive dissonance. If people see clearly who they are, and they see who they want to be, they will feel a need to close the gap. They have three choices at that point:

They can do nothing, resulting in some form of neuroses, or they can change their values to the level of their behavior. (A drug addict noting he would be more fulfilled living a sober life can say. "I like drug addicts. It is not such a bad thing to be an addict.) We call this rationalization.

They can lift their behavior to the level of their aspirations.
(We call this courage. Or grit.)

At first glance, this seems frightfully simple. It is not.

As we discussed earlier, it is very difficult for people to assess accurately where they are. How many diets have failed because the morbidly obese person says to him or herself, "I am not all that fat."

How many of us have encountered the man who all evidence to the contrary says, "I am not that grumpy", or "I don't drink that much."

Also, many people have not defined clearly where they want to be. The old expression, 'if you're not sure where you're going, any road will get you there", holds.

Fran counsels school principals and school superintendents professionally. In his practice, he works with people who manage multi-million-dollar budgets or sometimes hundreds of millions of dollars. He cannot believe how many of them have failed to develop a personal financial plan. Many wait until they are in their late 50s before they begin to think about how much money they will need in retirement.

Many over-rely on credit cards sometimes paying twice the value of what they bought over five years when interest is considered. They pay off that item, at a great cost, that they bought, because of a wonderful sale. How can people be experts in finance and budgeting and run their own finances so poorly?

They are not different from other people. Many of us repeatedly make this mistake. It is just surprising that people don't have a clear vision of where they are, and where they want to be, and a path of how they are going to get there.

Fran often makes the argument, to a disbelieving audience, that being rich is simply a decision a person has to make when they are young.

Ultimately, the small decisions make the difference. Daily, we choose between a tuna sandwich brought from home or a steak bought at a trendy restaurant. This and dozens of similar decisions contribute over 30 years to whether you have wealth, or whether you struggle through your last 10 years of life. If a person were clear about where they wanted to be financially and understood how their present behavior contributes to that outcome, they could achieve it.

Most people want to be rich. The problem is they also want to live the life of a rich man when they are not. The problem is that these can be competing interests. The odds are the lottery will not solve this problem for you.

In this country, we argue that we have a drug crisis. We have a shortage of investment capital. We have an obesity problem. We have too much alcoholism, too

138

many unwed mothers, too much juvenile delinquency, too much drunk-driving, and too much crime...In actuality, we have one problem. We have a decision-making crisis. When you don't know where you want to be and don't know where you are, any road will get you there.

Reframing can provide rare moments to help people locate themselves in the change process.

To improve customer relations, we need a clearer sense of where we are going and where we are now.

A reframing moment is a moment of singular clarity or insight. In that reframing moment, we see simultaneously where we are and where we want to be. It causes us to challenge our assumptions.

It is for a person, a group, or an organization, a time when we shift our thinking from a spiraling non-productive pattern to a new and more productive pattern. Often, the reframing moment requires a catalyst. A top-notch customer service person can reframe an issue for a customer and provide insight.

Questions:

1) Is confronting people about their inadequacies effective?

2) Why must reframing be done with a twinkle in the eye?

Chapter 13
Some Useful Examples of Reframing.

"Coming up sideways, in a startling way, allows the message to be heard."

In this chapter, we will provide stories of several reframing moments so that the reader can identify a reframing event when it occurs. Let's begin:

The grandmother had cornered the school principal. She was unhappy because her grandchild had reported to her about a few bad experiences with a teacher; we will call Ms. Smith. The grandmother first explained what happened in each of the incidents involving Ms. Smith.

The principal gently reminded the grandmother that

sometimes the stories told by grandchildren don't line up with the facts. She indicated that she would investigate the grandmother's concerns and would get back to the grandmother.

The grandmother was not entirely happy. "Did the principal know," the grandmother thought silently "that this was her precious grandchild? Did she know that this teacher was mean?" "How could she be so stupid?"

There was only one correct response for the principal to make from the grandmother's point of view. The principal was going to bang Ms. Smith over the head, symbolically, if not in actual practice. Grandma had to get this principal's mind right. The principal had some learning to do, and she would set the principal straight.

The grandmother told all the stories again. The principal thanked her and told her once again that she would speak to the teacher. The principal tried to bring the conversation to a close.

The grandmother was pretty clear that the principal did not fully understand her. If the principal did, the principal clearly would bang this teacher over the head. So, she proceeded to explain the stories again.

Have you ever been there, when a customer won't stop explaining the problem? You have budgeted 10 minutes for the encounter. You are a half-hour into it, and there is no end in sight!

Grandma decided to launch into the problems her grandchild had with other teachers earlier and scout troop leaders and....

The principal remembered in this encounter something he had learned from Fran, who first learned it from Sid in a seminar. The principal addressed the grandmother, "Do you mind if I get started on this right away? I've got some time available now and I would like to jump in on this problem right away."

(What was Grandma going to do? Could she say, "Yes, I mind? Don't get started on this right away." Of course, she wouldn't do that.)

Instead, she said, "No you go right ahead. I am

going to the store but I will be back home by three o'clock. Give me a call. Let me know what comes of it. Thank you, Madame Principal."

Why was this a reframing event? The grandmother viewed this encounter as a time she was needed to complain endlessly. She was concerned that no other behavior would get the result she wanted. Her continued complaining had worked in the past. Eventually, the people she complained to, got to it. She assumed it was the endless nature of her complaint that achieved her success. Big problems required big complaining.

Her view seemed to be that the more she complained, the more likely it was that the principal would go along with her. She was not sympathetic to the principal's need to investigate. (She already *knew* the facts.) She was unconcerned with the teachers' rights. It was her grandchild's rights that were important. Grandma was waiting to hear what kind of punishment the principal was going to deliver to the teacher and Grandma probably wanted her grandchild placed in another room.

She just ground people down. She was good at it.

This caused a real intellectual/emotional knot. The principal could not punish the teacher without investigating and finding a punishable offense. These situations are not always what they appear to be, the principal knew.

The encounter needed a new frame of reference. The principal provided it when she asked, "Do you mind if I get started on that right away?" Suddenly, the grandmother was reminded gently, (with a sort of twinkle in the principal's eye), that the principal needed time to resolve the problem; and, she the grandmother, was consuming too much of it. Grandma also knew that she was heard. The principal was going to do something. Grandma could relax until 3:00 PM.

As in most of these situations, other formulations of the question could also work. For example, the principal could have said, 'I have one hour in my schedule to work on this problem today, and perhaps even more tomorrow. How much more time should we spend helping me to better understand your perspective on the problem because that will have to come out of the time, I have to

145

work on it." The words themselves have no magic.

She did not confront the grandmother directly but asked a question with such simplicity and clarity, that the grandmother gained the insight that her behavior was interfering with the satisfactory resolution of the problem, and she let the principal go.

One of Sid's early experiments with reframing happened when he worked in an auto parts store. He had sold a man shock absorbers. The man went home to install them. Installing a shock absorber is dirty, time-consuming work, particularly when done at home without the benefit of a hydraulic car lift.

After several hours of dirty work, the new shocks were installed. When the man lowered the car from the jack stands, one of the newly installed shock absorbers buckled. There had been a defect in the shock absorber. He was angry and disgusted with the parts store, especially, his point of contact, the not-yet-famous Sid Hurlbert, then, simply another sales clerk.

The car was the man's only vehicle. To return the

shock absorber, the man had to put the vehicle back on the jack stands, crawl under the car, and reinstall the just removed older part to drive back to the parts store to get a replacement part.

When he entered the store, he was furious. He approached Sid seething with rage. Sid grabbed the defective shock absorber, spun on his heel, and said over his shoulder "Follow me."

As Sid strode purposely forward, the man shuffled behind. Sid walked first in one direction and then in another. He led the man on a merry chase.

To a casual observer, had there been one, it would have looked like a drum major swinging a broken shock instead of a baton bouncing about the store, in a very short parade, with an out-of-step band member who had left his instrument at home.

The client exploded in outrage. "What are you trying to pull?" Sid just grinned. Then the client began to laugh, seeing the absurdity of what had just happened. Sid smiled, and the twinkle in his eye allowing the man to know that they could have fun, even in a tense situation. Sid had taken an enormous risk. But the gamble resulted in a window of opportunity.

Sid said, "I am so sorry. I can see why you are so mad. I would be too. This should not have happened. Let me refund your money *and* give you a set of new shock absorbers. I will upgrade the quality as well. I will call a garage we work with to have them do the work for you right now at our expense."

I will drive you to wherever you would prefer to be while the work is done, and then pick you up again to get your car,

Outrageous problems require outrageous solutions.

Sid had not only retained a customer in a difficult situation but he had gained a friend.

Both men were in a very difficult situation. Who cannot relate to the anger of the customer? Yet, how else could Sid resolve the problem to the satisfaction of the customer?

If the man with the broken shock were a typical do-it-yourselfer, he had probably spent four hours installing the defective shock, then more time removing the defective "new shock," just to be able to drive back to the store. Now he feared he would have to uninstall the temporary worn shock he had already removed and reinstalled, simply to get back to the store. Now he would have to spend more time reinstalling the new one.

He had lost the better part of the day because the shock absorber he had bought was no good.

Yet, Sid did not manufacture the shock absorber, nor had the store had trouble with this brand before. Sid wasn't knowingly selling bad merchandise.

It was one of those problems that was bound to happen once in every ten thousand sales and this day it landed on Sid and this poor unsuspecting customer. Pobody is nerfect.

Would this solution always work? Maybe not! Could it work for anybody but Sid? Maybe not!

149

How could we reframe it and stay within our safety zone?

Try this: "Believe me I know how you must feel. My goal is to not just solve this problem but to delight you. I know that it is hard to imagine us delighting you after what has happened but give me a chance.   Here is an idea. Why don't we take you wherever you are going, we will keep your car, we will pay to have it fixed, we will refund the money you spent. We will upgrade your shocks to a better brand and we will give you a thirty-dollar credit in our store when we deliver your repaired car. I truly am truly sorry."

Extreme kindness in a crisis often lets people know we heard them and that we care about them and their business.   That alone can reframe a situation, often because the customer may be concerned, at that moment, that you neither heard nor cared.

Fran had such an experience at a local Lowes home improvement store.   Fran had ordered three new storm doors in April to use as screen doors in the summer. First, the store lost the order. Then, the doors came in, but they were the wrong size even though Lowes had measured the opening themselves. Then, Lowes lost the reorder. Then, the doors came in broken. Then, they forgot to reorder.

By October, Fran had lost it. He had gone all summer without any screen doors and now the cold was blowing through the unprotected doors. After having talked to store employees over and over, he scheduled a meeting with the store manager. The manager had researched the multiple foul-ups while waiting for Fran to drive in for his appointment. When Fran got to the store, the manager had reordered the doors in a rush order, scheduled an installation, and credited Fran's account with the $700 Fran originally spent on the three new doors.

Now, that is reframing a problem. Fran has been a regular customer at Lowes ever since.

Sid even uses reframing in his personal life. Sid loves his dad, who truly has a kindly heart. He is fundamentally a good man but he has a tongue that sometimes spirals out of control. Sometimes, his tongue can melt the skin off a turnip. He is like a lot of men, too often too grumpy.

Sid's mom is sweet as honey, sensitive, and long-suffering. Already, you the reader can anticipate some of the dramas that might take place in this home. Sid's dad, who genuinely loves his wife, but sometimes fires from the lip, at something unimportant. This sends his mom into genuine pain, causing discomfort for the whole family. This is a classic pattern for the many families with this problem.

A wall sometimes builds up between the father and the mother caused by the scarring due to this repeated pattern of behavior. The scar tissue built up to protect everyone's feelings builds a wall that is hard to penetrate.

The children will uncomfortably endure this friction, building resentment towards the father, and finally, the child may explode in anger toward the father to protect the mother.

This can, with the father's tendency to "blow off steam", result in a rebounding attack on the child, curiously by either the father or the mother. These kinds of dynamics often tear families apart. The problem is often aggravated because the child, in defending the mother, "attacks" the father's ego. The father's defenses surge, and, given his volatile nature... It is a classic "knot."

What is needed is reframing.

Lest the reader thinks this kind of family dynamics are unusual, they probably describe the family dynamics for between 25% and 40% of families.

Most of us probably owe the survival of our genetic line to the existence of an aggressive male ancestor, at some time, in the long history of our family. Fortunately, for most of us, such aggression is no longer needed or desired. But, as we have learned, old genetic tendencies did not arrive in a single day, nor will they disappear in a single day. (None of this discussion is meant to forgive such verbal violence, not to mention any explicitly illegal acts of physical violence.)

As a species, we have more funny genetic wiring than most of us are likely to admit. (Sid and Fran for example, tend to pack on the pounds.) Food was once scarcer in parts of the world than it is in America today. And when food was available, it could be a long time before it was available again.

The ability to store food energy as fat was a key to some of our ancestor's survival. That inherited trait is not working well for Fran or Sid right now, though. There are plenty of other examples of traits that our ancestors needed to be successful, that do not work as well for us today. However, genes are genes. They don't change quickly.

Sid had learned through bitter experience that confronting his dad every time that he barked at his mom was not an effective solution to the problem. Experience had taught Sid this. It felt good to confront his dad. Sid would be cloaked in righteousness every time he confronted his father. However, it neither improved his father's behavior nor did it improve Sid's family dynamics.

Sid's father knew, at some level that he was a grump. He didn't understand the mechanics of his personality that caused him to be this way, but he knew.

Sid wanted to have his father morph into Fred McMurray in "Father Knows Best", the kind and loving dad who never lost his temper. His dad couldn't admit that he was not the way he, himself wanted to be. Who wants to acknowledge, that sometimes they are mean to their family?

This is how defenses get in the way.

Sid's dad was not happy with his impatience, and his belittling behavior. Knowing this did not help, however. People confronted him with his behavior. In response, he would exercise his complete set of defensive behaviors, which usually were aggressive, making matters worse. He knew this too somewhere deep in his soul. But he could not seem to help himself.

Sid's dad had a clear vision of where he wanted to be. He just had a hard time seeing how the present moment was related to that vision. He needed to be reminded in a non-threatening way that his behavior was out of bounds. A confrontation ran the risk of bringing about the exact kind of behavior Sid was trying to overcome.

One day, Sid's parents were driving him to the airport. They live nearby and love to support Sid and his career. His mom and dad had organized quite a few happy errands around the trip to the airport.

After they dropped Sid, they were going to pay some bills, pick up some things they needed, and return home full of accomplishments. There was no time pressure after they dropped off Sid, but true to type, Sid's dad was self-pressured to move ahead briskly. He was on the edge of impatience, as they left the driveway.

About a mile from the house, Sid's mom began to shuffle through her purse. It was the kind of purse that Kansas could have been placed in and still have had room for Rhode Island. She shuffled through the purse for probably 45 seconds looking more and more worried, each second. Finally, Sid's dad exploded. "What are you doing?" he screamed.

Timidly, she muttered, "I think I left the checkbook home."

Sid's dad's face contorted with rage, "How could you be so stupid? You would leave your head home if it were not attached. I cannot believe..."

Sid's first instinct was to say, "I think I will get out here. It is eight miles to the airport but I think I can walk that far, carrying these two heavy bags and this projector". This was a classic flight response, from the old flight or fight responses that we have "wired-in".

His next impulse was to confront his dad head-on. His dad was out-of-line. This was a classic fight response. Moral indignation always feels good. Lecturing someone else about his or her bad behavior always gives us a sense of moral superiority.

However, it rarely works. It usually just raises the defensiveness of the person we have admonished. The problem becomes clearer for us if we pause for a moment to think about how we feel when someone else lectures us about our bad behavior.

These are very difficult situations. When a pattern has repeated itself for 30 or 40 years, responding to it, as you always have, is unlikely to bring any different results. Whether it is this pattern of behavior; or some other patterns of behavior, we often find ourselves playing out a drama not so different from this one. Sid has a highly developed ability to reframe problems for people. This time it would be different.

"Mom," Sid admonished, "How could you do this to dad? You are always doing this kind of thing. I saw you at home, slyly pulling your checkbook from that purse and hiding it under the lamp. Why do you do these things to dad?"

"Sid," his dad hollered in reply. "Your mother would do no such thing. How could you say such a thing? She wouldn't leave the checkbook home, on purpose." Sid's father paused... looked embarrassed... and began to laugh. He had just made Sid's point. Sid's dad was caught.

His dad realized instantly how stupid he had been for attacking his wife over this simple mental lapse. Yet, his defenses had not been raised. The older couple began to giggle like children in the front seat of the car. No further words needed to be said. The father had gained insight. He adjusted his attitude and had his temper in check, at least for this day.

Reframing can work at home as well as at work.

We hope these examples are beginning to form a pattern. Reframing brings insight, often in a potentially tense situation, by "coming up sideways" on a person, instead of hitting it "head-on". Here is another example.

Fran's mom had had rheumatic fever as a child. This resulted in a bad heart valve, which resulted in heart valve replacement surgery, which resulted in a series of strokes. Each stroke took a little bit away from his mom.

The word lamb, for example, could frequently be substituted for any word, whatsoever. It was, for her the "go-to" word. "Get me the lamb" could mean get me the car keys, get me my tea, or get me the TV guide.

159

Her ability to sequence simple steps in a familiar process disappeared. So, she would sometimes put the teabag in the cup, put the cup and tea bag together in the microwave for two minutes then add cold water. She lost her ability to understand time.

The relative position of events lost their meaning, entirely. Her balance was compromised. Her speech was badly affected. Even some of Fran's brothers and sisters could not understand what she was saying when she spoke.

The series of strokes presented all kinds of challenges to the entire family. Fran's dad, like Sid's, tended toward impatience. He genuinely loved his wife but was frustrated that some of the familiar patterns of their life were shattered by her disability.

Others could no longer see Fran's mom as an intellectual equal because of her inability to express herself. Speech, one of the ways we informally measure intelligence, had diminished dramatically.

The situation needed to be reframed. The family needed a metaphor to cope with the changes in their family that her health issues had caused.

"I've got it," Fran blurted aloud to no one in particular, "We will begin to think of her as a dotty British eccentric. You know how in those old movies; the older British aristocrats are always doing weird things. No one resents them for it. They just act weird and then carry the title of eccentric like it is a badge of honor. You know, "Come meet my mom, she is a little weird; but that is what is so cool about her. She is eccentric, not brain-damaged."

It didn't work for everyone in the family. Fran's dad continued to be too irritable. Others in the family found it to be more or less helpful. For Fran and his wife, Lisa, it was the key to their relationship with his mom. They didn't fall into the old traps of irritability, or condescension. Her last years on earth were among the best years for Fran's relationship with his mom. This was, purely, because the situation was reframed.

One final example:

One day while writing this book was a sunny Friday. Fran was working in the rear of the house by the pool. The neighbors had hired a pretty rough crew to paint their (the neighbor's) home.

All morning the painters had played a particularly gritty kind of rock and roll music at full volume. The music just did not improve the act of writing, for Fran.

Yet, this bunch would not have responded well to "turn that damned thing down," or "change the channel".
The dimensions of their defenses were unpredictable, at best. Fran was pulling out some of the last strands of what little hair he has left.

His wife Lisa is a natural reframer. She approached the painters, who were not nearly done with the paint job, and would be working late that day.

"Thanks for providing the soundtrack this morning," she said. 'I'd like to make the selections this afternoon. If you would turn your boom box down, I'll crank mine up. You can try my tunes this afternoon. At the end of the day, let's compare notes over a beer."

They turned their music off. Ella Fitzgerald replaced Def Leopard. The music for the rest of the day helped the writing. Her approach was far more effective than an approach that attacked their rock and roll. And the beer at the end of the day was fun for everyone.

Reframing sometimes is the only way to effectively resolve a problem, and, as you will soon see it can be the key to improving customer service.

Questions:

1) Are you beginning to find a pattern in the reframing examples?

2) How would you articulate that pattern?

3) Can you understand why a twinkle in the eye is needed to make this work?

Chapter 14

Awareness of when to risk reframing

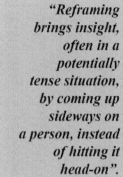

"Reframing brings insight, often in a potentially tense situation, by coming up sideways on a person, instead of hitting it head-on".

Some who read this book already have a gift for helping others to reframe difficult situations. Most of us could stand to improve our skills in this area.

The problem is that these are not skills, like long division, that can be easily taught in isolation, and then combined to make the student competent. We will, however, do our best to break the steps down to make success at reframing more probable. Much of the remainder of this book will attempt to analyze and teach the components of reframing and how to apply them.

Once you have tried reframing a few times successfully it can become a tool that you can count on.

Here are a few things to consider in trying out reframing:

We are alerted to the need to try something different. We have either tried to resolve this problem too many times before or our intuition just tells us it is time for a new approach

People don't need to reframe every decision that they face. Most of what we do in life is automatic, or nearly automatic, and that is great news. Deciding whether to use a fork or spoon to eat a cream soup should probably not require a tremendous amount of mental energy. There are, however, situations that call out for reframing.

Knowing when to use this tool is the first step. We need to learn to recognize those moments. There are always knots. These are complex problems, difficult to untie.

In our lives, there are many times that our logic becomes circular and we get a bad result. An example taken from the parenting of teens might be helpful here.

Teenagers sometimes fall into a cycle of bad behavior. This usually starts innocently enough when a teenager hits a mild bump in the road, like getting a bad grade on a report card. As loving parents, we might impose limits on our child in response. We might tell a teenager in such a bind that they are grounded for two weeks.

The teenager, feeling bad about the report card result and for having disappointed mom and dad, might also be angry because they can't, now, see their boyfriend/girlfriend. A fight response might kick for the teen from the old fight or flight tape. To strike back, the teen might not come home from school one day, go to a friend's house, and return home only to face a new punishment which might then cause them to be grounded for a month.

The teen's frustration and anger might trigger them to swear at their parent, which could result in them being grounded for another month. (Fight or flight). The frustration and anger from the incidents above might cause them to smuggle alcohol into the house, and….

No parental response in the above example was wrong by itself. Kids need limits. We agree that behaviors should lead to consequences, positive and negative. Consistency is important.

But, oops! Something went wrong here. However logical, kind, and thoughtful, the parents in this story may have thought themselves to be, this situation is going nowhere.

This is a classic knot. The patterns that we use to solve problems are not working and are getting us nowhere. The two lines are bound up in a knot and it is hard to find a loose end to untie it.

This situation screams for reframing. This is not a book on parenting. This section is to help you how to identify when reframing is needed.

In this case, the parents used a common remedy for a real problem that has been used repeatedly by others. It simply has not worked. Soon the rebellion, at hand, is going to boil over.

Some parents would just continue to punish the teen into compliance. Could it work? It is a test of wills. We see a pattern. Certainly, there is a risk in simply applying the same solution, which has not gotten results.

Fran raised a lot of children, not all of whom were his own. As a school superintendent, he was often in a position to catch kids, who were in a free fall. He used to buy Monopoly games at garage sales just to remove the "get out of jail free" card to use when punishment failed to get results.

Sometimes he needed to break through this vicious cycle which was: Bad behavior causes punishment which causes resentment, causing more bad behavior, which causes more punishment, causing more resentment, which causes more bad behavior which causes more punishment, causing bad behavior, which causes, etc.

The opportunity to issue a get out of jail free card was a chance to reset. It offered both sides the opportunity for redemption. The offending behavior could be reconsidered outside the cycle of retribution.

169

When you are doing some things repeatedly that does not work, do something else.

These knots or puzzles happen more frequently than you might imagine. Sometimes they represent lifelong patterns of behavior. When someone is trapped in one of these knots, their ability to choose an effective new behavior from a wide repertoire of behaviors diminishes.

When involved in one of these situations, one gets the sense that they are in a scene that was written by someone else. Like, in any good knot, there seems to be no place to reach in and pull the strands apart.

What does this have to do with customer service?

We have used several examples in the last few pages that are readily identifiable as knots or puzzles. Do you remember the case of the grumpy waitress? Sid went into a restaurant for breakfast. The waitress came over and snarled a surly "What do you want?" Her mannerisms were hostile. The experience was unpleasant.

Her behavior made perfect sense to her. She never

had her behavior meaningfully challenged. Her thinking was loosely based on contempt for her work and her customers. The poor tips she received reinforced that her customers were "scum." There was no reason to adjust her thinking. There was an internal logic, "I may have to wait on these people but I don't have to like it."

The internal logic propelled the behavior. It was like a drama written by someone else. The actual logic of her behavior was counterproductive.

A more productive logic ought to have been, "I work for tips; I ought to 'suck up' to these people." Or, "it is a privilege to serve people." Or, "I can make their day." Or, "Through my outstanding service, I can make this company thrive." Or, "If I am kind and helpful, people will love me and I will be happier." These thoughts never crossed her mind. She was trapped in a knot of her own making.

From the outside, we can all see that the logic of these other pieces of "self-talk" would simply work better for the waitress. If she could learn to value customer service and permit that value to change her behavior, her job would be more secure. Her boss would be happier. She would get more tips. Her days would fly by. Her work would feel lighter.

She would be happier. Not only, would this commitment to personal service, bring new customers, but it could also provide her constant "strokes". She would get great feedback. As Sid has said earlier in the book, "The most important reason to give great customer service is that it feels good."

This woman has her logic clearly in a knot. Her attitude has imprisoned her from seeing reality. Sid's reframing remark, "I'll have another waitress" came up along her sideways. It alerted her to the problem without raising her defenses.

The guy with the shock absorber was also about to enter a huge knot. Remember him, from earlier in the book? He was a do-it-yourself mechanic who bought a shock absorber from Sid. When he installed it, it buckled.

He had to put the old one back on to drive to the store to get a replacement. This doubled the time he had in the project. And he still had a broken shock. He didn't know how Sid would handle it. Faced with overwhelming disappointment and unhappiness, old tapes from infancy began to take over his behavior.

When an infant is tired, hungry, sick, cold, hot, sore, wet, or lying-in fecal material, the infant responds with a generalized body spasm. It is often involuntary. He or she becomes wracked with tears.

Over time, children learn that this generalized response also brings a generalized and non-specific response from the adult. Tears over a safety pin stuck in the infant's side can bring a warm bottle of milk instead of the relief the infant seeks. So, children learn, over time, to be more specific about what concerns them; and to approach the adults using methods that bring them the results they want more effectively.

However, when faced with profound disappointment the old tapes often play in our heads, and we respond like an infant, merely expressing our pain with a generalized full-body response.

The customer could have been more effective by raising his concerns differently. "Sid, I have just had an experience that is so painful to me, that I am likely to behave rather badly. Sid, think of yourself as a contestant in the national customer service quiz show. You need an A+ response on this customer service challenge to move into the million-dollar round...Are you ready Sid? I've got one heck of a story for you."

He did not. He was just poised to go crazy.

Had the customer done what was described above this would have been an example of the customer reframing the situation for the customer service representative. And, it might have worked.

The point is that the old tape, the infancy whine, is not particularly productive. It often creates an example of a knot or puzzle that calls out for reframing.

In response to name-calling and accusations, the customer service professional may become defensive. Now the crisis has been made worse.

So, the first step in using reframing effectively is to understand when to use it. We don't use it to handle everyday routine problems. Life should not demand that kind of creativity and mental energy every minute of every day. Reframing provides people with an opportunity to see a complex problem from a fresh perspective.

People, groups, or organizations can be "stuck" in a non-productive bit of circular reasoning. Sometimes they will exhibit behaviors that make sense to them but don't make sense. They may be in a knot that would benefit from reframing.

When people are locked in a non-productive self-reinforcing set of behaviors that simply don't work, reframing may be helpful. That is why we say, "Caution signals alert us, indicating that this is a problem that calls out for reframing." Knowing when to use reframing is the first step to using it effectively.

Quotes:

"When you are doing some things repeatedly that

do not work, do something else."

"In our lives, there are many times that our logic becomes circular, and we get a bad result."

Questions:

1) Have you ever been caught up in the kinds of knots described here?

2) Would a fresh approach that did not attack you have been useful then?

3) Without the training in reframing, did you ever reframe a situation before? Did it help?

Chapter 15

Reframing is Built on Understanding the Problem

Once people understand what they want and understand where they are now, they can opt to close the gap. The actual problem is often quite different from the problem presented. Reframing can help focus on the true issue without causing people to raise those pesky defenses.

Understanding the underlying dynamics of the situation is worth spending some time to sort out.

The diabetic woman came into a discount department store late in the evening. She was quite frantic. She asked a clerk to replace her defective glucometer. (The glucometer is a portable electronic device that measures sugar in the blood.) The clerk was certainly willing to help and went to his computer to enter the return.

A note came up on his computer screen indicating that because this product used blood samples, it could not be returned.

"I can do nothing about this tonight the repair service is closed and I cannot override the computer." he said.

Behind the clerk, above the counter, was a blue sign that stated all defective products sold at this store, would be cheerfully replaced or repaired by the company.

The conversation that followed was predictably ugly. The diabetic kept pointing to the sign. The clerk kept saying that he was not permitted to return this product without approval from the computer. She began to rant and rave about a store run by a computer. Could she have a word with the computer? Customers were beginning to gather. They surrounded the two who were locked in a crisis, with all the enthusiasm of fans at a prizefight.

They gathered in a rough semicircle to enjoy the clamor unfolding before them. The horror unfolding before them did not disappoint. The manager of the store was drawn by the commotion.

He approached the scene confidently, extended his hand to the customer, and said, "I am Neil Rochelle. I am the manager of the store. May I help you?"

"I hope so," she fired back. "This sorry-ass shit-for-brains clerk can't read his own damned sign. It says we will fix or replace any broken stuff. I bought this glucometer today when my old one wore out. I have the receipt. It never worked, not once. I need a new one right now."

This was a critical moment. Neil knew that. The crowd had gathered, the employee wanted to be supported, the woman seemed in crisis. Neil's first instinct was to give this woman a lesson about her foul mouth. His blood pressure had immediately gone up, because of her assault on his employee. The clerk was not a brain surgeon, but he was a nice enough kid.

Everywhere there is an "us and them" mentality.

In this case, the "us" was the store employees and "them" were the customers. Neil could already see that this well-worn approach defending the clerk was going to go nowhere. He knew that his instinctive response to defend the kid was only going to escalate the crisis and cause further problems. Caution signals had gone up. He was now seeking to understand what is driving the present difficulty.

"What is a glucometer?" he asked innocently.

"It is a thing-a-ma-bob I use to measure my blood sugar," she replied.

"Are you a diabetic?" Neil asked. "Yes, damn it!" she spurted

"That must be difficult," Neil sympathized.

"You have no idea," she said. She breathed a little easier. At last, someone was listening.

"So help me to understand what is going on?" he asked in a concerned voice. (Not a bad opener in a crisis.)

"My sugar levels have been bouncing all over the place. I thought it was me, but when my old glucometer finally crapped out, I began to wonder if the glucometer had been the problem. So, I bought this new one today. Before I even was able to test my blood sugar one time, it turned up busted, and this jerk told me I can't return it. I spent all I had on it. I'm stuck, and I am worried about my blood sugar. I have not had a reading I could trust in weeks. I could be in real trouble with no way to find out. If I could get an accurate reading, I could either take some insulin to lower my sugar or eat some candy to raise it."

The required level of understanding had now been achieved. Neil had dug a little deeper than the clerk had. He knew now, what the underlying dynamic was. Two people were now talking. They were no longer two adversaries. Neil had connected with the customer. Neil had the opportunity to solve the problem now.

"What is your name?" Neil asked. He was moving away from the adversarial relationship further and toward a more cordial one.

"Ruth", she said.

"Ruth, he addressed her, "Peter here is not a bad kid. He is certainly not a   jerk.   We don't get problems like this very often, and frankly, we are going to learn from this one and change our policy." However, I am more concerned about your health right now. You need to get an accurate reading tonight. Don't you?"

"Yes", she said with a sense of relief. She had finally been heard.

"Peter, you go get Ruth a new one of these off the shelf, unless you would rather have a different brand, Ruth", Neil asked.

"No", Ruth said thoughtfully. "I have been reading about these, I think I just got a defective one."

The people, who had gathered for the show, were drifting away.

"Once you have the new glucometer, we will give it to Ruth. Ruth, I don't know how we will sort this out tomorrow, but I want you to hold the bad one, too. Bring the bad one back tomorrow, and we will figure out what to do with it.

I will be in at noon and I will call headquarters right away to sort out what we will do. They are not open tonight. I will work until closing tomorrow night. You can come in any time after 1:00 PM. We may end up sending it back to the company, but I will know that tomorrow before you get here.

These things are so reliable that we have never had this come up before. I am sure Peter agrees with me, the most important thing we can do tonight is to make sure you get the information you need to manage your diabetes, right, Peter?"

"Absolutely," Peter responded.

By now, the last of the assembled crowd had left. If anything, Ruth had become a more committed customer. Peter felt supported, and Neil was able to go home feeling good about himself, his company, and the level of service he had provided. He had a story about work to tell his wife and children. The reason for all of this good feeling came from his ability to understand the underlying dynamic, not merely the presenting dynamic.

It was presented as an "us vs. them" power struggle about company regulations and policies, but it was a health crisis, resolved by an empowered and understanding employee.

"Seek first to understand, then to be understood."

This story is beautiful; however, it is not true. In the true story, Fran, our author, was Ruth. No manager appeared. The computer was in charge, and with blood sugar screaming out of control at 9:55 PM with no other possibility to buy a glucometer that night; he left the store with no resolution to his health problem.

Fran never shopped in this store again.

The crowd that gathered around the explosive vignette probably contained a few people, who, horrified at the apparent insensitivity of the store policy also stopped shopping there.

Like most wronged customers, Fran proceeded to tell the story to his friends, students, colleagues, and relatives with increasing emotion. Some probably reduced their frequency of shopping at the store.

The reason for the store's policy probably makes sense. Who wants to accept returned products with the potential for dirty needles?

But, diligent adherence to what may seem to be a reasonable policy, in this case, was indefensible.

Organizations must not only do the right thing, but they must do what appears to be the right thing, and that is a higher standard. Any time your brain is screaming that this is an absurd result, find another solution. You do not want your well-meaning behavior to be at the heart of someone's story about insensitive treatment. And you want to go home feeling you did a good deed that day.

Even Fran would agree that handling other people's dirty needles is a bad idea; and that generally, glucometers are very reliable. This problem is quite rare, and I am sure the store sees the problem almost never, and probably never at closing time. Perhaps, it is the only time it has ever happened.

In the true story, all parties lost. No one reframed the issue. No one attempted to understand. Fran's blood remained undiagnosed and untreated.

The next day, Fran called the manufacturer of the glucometer. He mailed it back to them, and they overnighted a new one in anticipation of the receipt of the broken glucometer. He bought a second one from a local drug store to fill the gap. He happily paid more than the discount department store price, rather than returning to that store to buy a second one. He now has a spare.

The store lost probably $5,000 in gross sales each year from Fran alone, not including the damage that he spread, by telling the story to others. Wouldn't it be nice if Neil actually existed and truly understood?

Even Neil Rochelle cannot resolve every situation. Sometimes customers are just plain crazy. (let's hope Fran is not.) Sometimes there is no solution.

Here is another problem with a happy ending achieved through understanding: Fran teaches at a college. A foreign gentleman was pacing back and forth outside his open door loudly huffing and grumbling as Fran was trying to teach on the first Saturday of the summer session in May.

Fran started the students on a case study; left the classroom, gently closed the door, and asked the man if he could help him. The man exploded in rage. "Where is the graduation?" the man asked in a heavily accented voice. "This is Saturday, today is graduation. Where is it?"

"What graduation?" Fran asked gently.

"This is St. John Fisher College, isn't it?" the man asked....

"Yes?" Fran said cautiously.

"My son said graduation was today," the man asserted.

Graduation had been the previous weekend. It had been a glorious affair. St. John Fisher College does graduations well. There were balloons, and speeches, and food in abundance. There was a sea of happy faces.

Fran wondered how this poor guy could have gotten his dates wrong. Did he come from out-of-town to attend graduation on the wrong weekend? Fran thought to himself, "Poor son-of gun. He missed a good one."

"No sir, graduation was last week."

"How could that be?", he asked. "My son told me it was today."

"I am very sorry you missed it. It was a great

occasion. Did your son graduate?" asked Fran seeking to understand. The caution light had already lit up.

"No, he did not. That is the problem. He was supposed to graduate. He has been coming to this college for four years, and he was supposed to graduate. This place always gives me the runaround."

I have come here to finally track down somebody who can tell me why he is not graduating. He says it is because he got a C minus on one course and the College is making him come back for an additional year. This College is so stupid. How could they do that to my boy?" he hollered shaking with rage.

Soon, the students in Fran's class would be finished with their review of the case study.

This was an enormous problem that would require hours to resolve. It was unraveling unpleasantly in the hallway outside Fran's room. This encounter took place at about 11:00 AM. The class that day would last until at least 3: OO PM.

It would do no good to explain to this gentleman that the college was a good place, that the college took excellent care of its students, and that the problem was probably more complex than the man was led to believe.

Instead, Fran reached into his wallet, brought out a business card, and said to the man, "My name is Dr. Murphy, I teach here. You have come to the right place. Let's work on this together. Let's try to find out what went wrong. We will need access to your son's records and he will have to provide us that access. Come to my office. We will write a release that will permit you and me to review his records.

"Bring your son on Monday with the release at 11:00 am to this office and we will go together to the registrar's office to find out what happened. If something outrageous has happened to your son, I will go with you to the proper College official's office and we will straighten it out. I will set up an appointment at the President's Office, in case we need it," Fran concluded.

A lot more needed to be done to fully understand the problem. But the problem, as presented, "Where's the graduation ceremony?" was not the problem. The problem was that this man felt the College had unfairly denied his son his diploma.

Fran did not respond to the problem presented. Instead, he addressed the underlying problem. Fran knew that there was more to the situation than the dad understood. Fran suspected that the man's son had been misleading him. He could not untangle that situation today.

But he could show the father that the College was not insensitive and that he, the father, was not without resources, or support from the College. The father left, confident that the situation would be resolved, with a plan of action. At last, he had been heard.

Of course, later the father would learn from the Registrar's Office that the student had failed numerous courses and also failed to tell his father the truth. The subsequent meetings were fascinating. The father's respect for the College was restored. The boy had a lot of explaining to do.

The problem presented, is sometimes not the actual problem. The first step in this process was to seek to understand what the issue was.

The two presenting situations in this section (the diabetic, in the first incidence; and, the angry father in the second) called out for a different response than an ordinary one. A bell should have gone off in the head of the person with the customer service opportunity, to more deeply understand this problem.

Without this deeper level of awareness, progress may not have been made. The old tapes would run. It is a critical step in the reframing process.

It shouldn't take a crisis for a company to push the "seek to understand" button. There are more systemic reasons for companies to use their instinct to understand the needs and desires of the customer at a profound level.

Jack Helfrich was Superintendent of Schools in the Kenmore-Tonawanda School District in suburban Buffalo, New York. He was celebrated for the high level of achievement of his school district. He was selected as the first New York State Superintendent of the Year, and won New York Stare Excelsior Award for quality, competing based on an institutional commitment to quality against New York's many other enterprises including those in the for-profit sector.

Jack had a lot of "secrets" to his success. One was very simple and very effective. Each of his managers (principals, assistant principals, assistant superintendents, and the superintendent himself) were tasked with the responsibility to call five "customers" every week, selected at random from the list of parents in the school system. They asked the same two questions every week. The conversation went as follows:

"Good morning, Mrs. Smith." This is Jack Helfrich. "I am the school superintendent here in Kenmore-Tonawanda, and, first, there is nothing wrong with Tommy. I am not calling with bad news of any kind."

"I try to call five parents a week to get parents' ideas of how we are doing, and how we could improve. Do you have a few minutes to talk today?"

(First of all, how is Jack doing? Has he impressed Mrs. Smith already? Has your child's superintendent called you this week to seek your feedback about how to improve the school system? Has his approach already startled Mrs. Smith with his commitment to customer service?)

"I have a few minutes," Mrs. Smith might say tentatively.

"How are we doing in support of Tommy's education?" Jack would ask. After her reply, Jack would follow up, "Are there ways that we could serve your family or Tommy better? Do you have any suggestions for ways we could improve? Are there things we are doing well that we ought to enhance? Is there something we are doing now that we could do more of? Do you have any other thoughts for us?"

After completing the conversation and taking notes throughout, Jack would thank Mrs. Smith for sharing her ideas and providing ways that the school system could improve. The notes from all the administrators would be

194

submitted in rough form every week to Jack's assistant where they would all be typed, distributed to the administrative team, and would become the first item of business on the administrative team's meeting agendas.

The time commitment on this task was minimal. Each administrator had to make one call a day. Jack's assistant spent about two hours each week collecting and typing the notes. Each month about one-half hour to forty-five minutes was devoted to understanding "the welcome voice of the customer." The benefits were enormous. To the point being made here, Jack knew he first had to understand.

Questions:

1) Does your organization give you enough authority to resolve customer concerns?

2) Do you think people in customer service roles take enough time to define the problem and understand customer concerns?

Chapter 16

Startle the Customer
with a Fresh Approach.

"What has value in this organization is not the goods on our shelves but the worth of the relationships with our customers."

The two fundamentals of reframing are that you "come up alongside" someone instead of hitting him or her head on; and, "to think outside the box"

There is a discipline to creativity. Here is an example:

Fran used to enter the National Pun Contest every year. To do that he had to be able to write an extended pun. At first, this seemed a daunting challenge. But, writing a pun is easier once you develop a system.

Most puns end after a long story with a sometimes

slightly mangled popular expression. So, Fran always began with a popular expression. Here is one of his best or worst of his puns, depending on your point of view:

Edgar Allen Poe was a great writer. He also used a lot of drugs. During his time, "laughing gas" was invented. Poe was dying to try it. So, he arranged to buy a balloon full of laughing gas for two hundred dollars. The night for the delivery came. The dealer of laughing gas came to the house with a tuba case. Inside the tuba case was to be a balloon full of laughing gas. Poe was to inhale the laughing gas from the balloon. Poe paid the man two hundred dollars. The man opened the tuba case but the balloon had burst. The gas had escaped.

Poe snatched back his money and said, "Do not gas Poe.

Do not collect two hundred dollars."

Isn't it amazing that Fran did not get even an honorable mention for that groaner? Aren't puns supposed to make dad jokes seem funny?

How did he write it? What is the insider's system for writing puns? He began with the monopoly expression "Do not pass go. Do not collect two hundred dollars. He was prepared to trade some letters around to make it work and wanted to write a story that would get him to that punch line. That is how you write a pun. You begin with the punch line and make up a story that will get you there.

Given a half bottle of bourbon and three idle hours, almost anyone can do it. Creativity often seems like a mysterious act. It is not. A careful reading of this section will help you be more systematic about your creativity.

How does one startle oneself with a fresh approach to a seemingly intractable problem?

Of course, you begin by being alert to the situation, and then you seek to understand the true dynamics underlying the problem. Now the creative work begins. Creativity is merely the combination of two or more things that are not ordinarily combined.

199

Let's review some of the examples we have already used. When the waitress approached Sid, to ask rudely, "What do you want?" Sid's "alert" signal already went off. He knew that this woman was locked in a frequently repeated pattern. He also knew he did not want to continue to support it. His "understanding" was immediate. This is a grumpy lady who does not want to help me. His "startle" response was quite simple. He took her question literally. "What do you want?"

"I want a new waitress."

There are many times that this approach works very easily. Waitresses often ask upon delivering the entrée, "will there be anything else."

Fran often replies, "Just your friendship and support."

When people respond to a question, as if they had never heard it before, they often startle people. We have automatic responses to certain questions. Any alternative reply brings freshness to the situation.

"How are you today?" someone asked Sid.

"Better than I deserve to be", Sid replies frequently.

"How are you today?" someone asks Fran.

"I am having more fun than I have pockets to put it in", Fran sometimes replies.

Sometimes, just taking a fresh approach to the ordinary routines of life will startle people into a new perspective. Sometimes in response to the same question "So how are you?" Fran sometimes replies, "Compared to whom?" Even responding to a routine question in a novel way causes people to stop and think.

How do these help people reframe? As a society, we are awash in pessimism.

Taking the mind out of park, and putting it into gear is often enough to cause everyone in the neighborhood to look freshly at the things that are going on in their lives. Fun is infectious. People catch it from one another and pass it around. One person can make a difference simply by startling people with fresh replies to common questions. It can be an alert that you are entering a "fun zone."

Novel replies to commonplace inquiries are not the only way to startle. Here is a second approach that like the earlier system for writing puns can be made to be a systematic approach to startling others. Analogies and metaphors are useful to find a fresh approach. Here is a customer service example:

The dapper gentlemen entered the downtown shoe store. He was wearing a brown suit and white and brown wing-tipped saddle shoes. His selection of tie and shirt were stunningly fashionable.   He was carrying a plastic bag with the name of the shoe store on it. In the bag, was a shoebox. He walked briskly to the counter. Moments later, a clerk moved behind the counter and said, "May I help you."

" Yes," the dapper gentlemen replied. "I brought these back. They don't fit. I would like to return them."

The clerk opened the box, pulled the shoes out, and coolly examined them. They were quite used. The heels were worn down enough so that a fussy person would have had them re-heeled. The soles were badly scuffed and worn. There were creases behind the toe cap that revealed a high level of use.

An alert went off in the sales clerk's mind that he was about to hit a place where an old tape would replay. The clerk had been through this situation many times. He knew that the store owner would not accept a worn pair of shoes to be put back into stock. The owner could not sell a pair of worn shoes. Therefore, could not take them back. The clerk knew that the scene was about to become ugly. "These shoes are badly worn," he would say.

"No, they are not," would come the reply. The clerk had an understanding of the underlying dynamics.

"Yes, they are", the clerk would reply.

"I am insulted", the man would say. "Are you saying I am trying to deceive you?"

What was needed now was a way to take a fresh approach, to *startle*.

"No wonder you stay in such great shape," the clerk noted. "Those clothes hang off of you beautifully. I saw when you walked in, you looked good. Your tailor must smile when he sells you a suit."

"Why, thank you," the gentlemen replied.

"You must be an exercise walker. Is that how you stay in such good shape?"

"Well yes that, and I go to the gym."

"Even though these shoes are almost new, I can't take them as a return because you are such an athletic gentleman. Your very personality wears down shoes faster than most men. I could offer you a discount on your next pair of shoes to compensate you for the inconvenience of these not fitting as well as they should."

"Well, thank you, young man. That would be very nice," the gentleman said.

A head-to-head confrontation rarely works to the satisfaction of both parties. Defenses get in the way.

Which of us, when we are customers, wants to be told we are lying (even when we are)?

The man had worn the shoes too much to return them. The owner would not accept used shoes back. By distracting the customer with some flattery, the clerk was able to "come up sideways" on this man instead of head-on. What could have been an ugly confrontation with a customer became pleasant by startling him. It is a good way to take the ego defenses out of the conversation.

Startling the customer is not just a way to reframe a customer complaint, but ought to be how we do business. As was pointed out earlier in the book, customer service is not a merely reactive response to customer unhappiness but ought to be a proactive and ongoing, method of engaging the customer in verbal and nonverbal ways. Customer service should also influence what we offer as well as how we offer it.

There has been a lot of talk in the management

literature over the past two decades about exceeding customer expectations. The Chrysler minivan must have more cup holders, per square inch than any car that we have ever seen. In Fran's family, there is a minivan and a Volvo. Fran is addicted to coffee. His wife Lisa shares this addiction. They love the cup holders in their mini van

If dramatically exceeding customer expectations is the essence of pleasing customers who crave coffee then Chrysler should lead the pack.

. When it came time to replace the Volvo, there was a spirited debate around the kitchen table.   The arguments for the Volvo were safety and Volvo's legendary durability.   The advocate at that table for another kind of car pushed the cup holders. (Fortunately, the Volvo XC90 had done a better job with cup holders than the older Volvo models.)   They ended up with a Volvo, much to Fran's delight.

A feature that "delighted" the customer like cup holders that was invented out of whole cloth, became a new essential ingredient? In 1970, none of us knew what a cup holder was. By 2020, cup holders had become a key criterion by which we select cars, a new minimum expectation.

Delighting the customer and exceeding expectations is how an organization brings the "startle" aspect of customer service into product design. But exceeding expectations is a never-ending challenge because customer expectations, as we saw in the Volvo example, raise with each improvement to the product or service.

In 1952, none of us "needed" air conditioning in a car. Air conditioning for most people in that era was rolling down the windows or lowering the convertible top. Radios, in 1952 were something we had at home, predominantly. Now, most of us "need" premium audio systems in our cars.

Startling the customer with our customer service takes work, originality, and focus.

Fran always pays too much for his groceries. As in many major markets, there are many places to buy groceries in western New York. The chain that has the best lighting, best displays, and best-trained employees is widely believed to charge a bit more for most of what it sells.

Yet Fran won't shop anywhere else. He drives right by a store from a competing chain, which, arguably, is cheaper, to get to "his" store. The chain he favors has people to help load the groceries into the car. Fran has never used their help, but he thinks it's "cool." If ever he needed them, they would be there. They spend more time on making attractive displays. The stores are as clean as we wish hospitals were. The lighting is perfect (Cher visited Rochester and approached the manager of one of these markets to ask that they open a store in her area.) Wegmans, a Rochester favorite grocery chain, is addicting.

A company that "leads" with its customer service can be outrageous. At a recent stay at a hotel, the Madison Renaissance, in Seattle, Fran called down to ask for a wake-up call. The telephone operator asked, "And, how would you like your morning coffee, Dr. Murphy?"

First, it was startling that she replied with Dr. Murphy. Fran does not wear his Ph.D. like armor. He had not registered as Dr. Murphy. The desk clerk must have picked it up from the credit card, and transmitted that info to the telephone operator. Fran replied, "That is a little personal, isn't it? Why do you care how I take my coffee?"

"We need to know how you like your coffee so that 5 minutes before you receive your wake-up call we can deliver a pot of steaming coffee outside your door so that you can wake up to coffee and the newspaper...or would you prefer some tea?"

Fran made it complicated. "I will have regular and my wife will have decaf and cream, please."

The next morning the Murphy's awoke, There was a small tray containing two full pots of coffee, one labeled regular and one decaf outside their door. There also was a newspaper and a flower in a bud vase and a carafe of cool cream.   Fran will not stay at another hotel in Seattle. This startling free service has become a new minimum expectation, at least, while staying in Seattle.

What did this uncommon service cost the hotel?

What percentage of the $250 per night charge was the expense of this startling service? Why wouldn't every hotel do this? What would it do for the mood of their customers, the morale of their staff, and the percentage of repeat business? How complicated is that?

Staff members providing extraordinary service love the response they get from customers. It propels further acts of world-class service. The Madison Renaissance is a place where outrageous acts of service are the norm for employees.

Camp Good Days and Special Times is a wonderful Rochester area camp for children and families with cancer. (It also serves families affected by Aids, violence, the death of a parent, burn victims, and …) Fran has been a long-time volunteer. If any organization was to be committed to exemplary customer service, this organization should be.

Gary Mervis, the founder of the camp, clearly understood this. He ensured that the mostly volunteer staff was selected and programs were designed to pack a "lifetime of fun in a single week". What does this level of customer service look like?

The commitment to children served by the camp (which is largely staffed by volunteers) results in a culture that has many startling features. Here are a few of the startling occurrences that have happened:

- When a bus arrives from a city served by the camp the staff is waiting to applaud the arrival of the new campers. The staff brings cheers and hugs in abundance, and hands to carry luggage to the welcoming cabin.

- Among the staff, the greatest honor is often to be the last served on the food line. Some of the staff are needed to eat with children, who require their company, and assistance. They line up with the children they are to serve. But, at Camp Good Days if you are the last to eat, it means you have given everyone else what they need first. That is a good thing. It is valued in that culture. How different is this from schools, whose teachers routinely cut in line?

- When waiting in line for dinner, lunch, or breakfast, strange things break out, like the back-scratching activity where each person, in line, scratches the back of the person in front of them.

- The program offerings have been infinite in their variety. We don't have a bowling alley and we don't offer a program in bowling. But, if any child mentions that they would like to go bowling, we arrange it, immediately. So, it is with airplane rides, hot air balloons, skin diving….

Top-quality customer service is by definition, not usual and customary. It does delight the customer. It catches the customer by surprise. It does startle.

How does a company or an organization move into this brave new world?

Let's go to the system we have already begun to develop. The first step was to be alert to the need for some special effort. The effort here, in developing a systematic startling, high level of customer service is knowing that if you don't exceed your customer's service expectations, you may be out of business. The second step was to understand the underlying dynamics by understanding customers' expectations, wants, desires, and needs.

Corporations and organizations that do this better than their competition are constantly and systematically engaged with their customers.

We may have it wrong, but we believe that Chrysler invented the cup holder. If so, they did not do that in isolation. They met with customers asking the customers to think "outside of the box".

"What bugs you as you drive to work in the morning?" They asked. "What would a car do that would delight you?" "If a car company could read your mind, what would be different about their product?"

"Would you mind if I ride with you everywhere you go, for a few days, to watch how you use our product?" "Any time you have a minor annoyance anywhere you go today, just tell me. We are trying to reinvent the whole experience of "car". Engineers would ask customers these kinds of questions.

How sophisticated does this research have to be? How many customers do you have to ask? Do you have to hire someone to do this research?

Some data is better than none. That's the bottom line. If you don't ask, you won't know.

Huge national advertising campaigns are tested on focus groups of no more than 10 or 20 people. People's views, although they vary, are more alike than they are dissimilar. A small group of customers can help companies gain new insights.

We were not insiders with Chrysler on the invention of the cup holder. Our fantasy is that some engineer was talking to a customer or riding with a customer in their car when the coffee spilled and the customer said," Damn, I hate it when my coffee mug spills when I turn suddenly." If someone had asked my father in 1952 about how he used his car and what his problems were and what annoyed him when he drove, a cup holder would have been in the 1953 Ford.

If an organization wants to startle their customers systematically, proactively, they will understand the customer's expectations, needs, wants, and the customer's minor annoyance with their products or services.

Would you like a tissue dispenser built into the cockpit of your car or automatic backup assistance especially designed for when you are backing up a trailer?

Great customer service does not just happen, nor will exhortations to improve customer relations do it alone. A company that exceeds the expectations of its customers has to want to exceed those expectations.

They have to hire people who want to do it. They have to want to provide customers with special experiences. It helps when they train their staff and then plan specifically how exceeding customer expectations will happen. Startling your customer in a world-class fashion is improved by a world-class organization, focused on the customer.

Mike Cobb when he worked at Great Peak Ski Area

understood this. He knew from talking to customers that waiting in line for the lift was one of the most annoying aspects of skiing.

He also knew by observing that the lines were worst from about ten o'clock in the morning until eleven-thirty, and then from one o'clock until about two-thirty. (The problem mostly existed on the weekends and holidays.)

He knew that at his ski area the real problem was at the main lift from his base lodge to the top of the mountain. The lifts at the side trails were not often crowded. (These observations were the most important part of finding solutions.)

If waiting in lines on all lifts, at all times, was the problem, there probably was no solution short of reducing the number of customers. But by understanding the problem in this way, the problem was more bite-sized.

The economics of that ski area did not support a second ski lift to parallel the main lift. Providing ticket prices that incentivized people to ski at off-peak hours had helped, but had not solved this problem. Mike asked himself, could he make the time spent waiting less irksome.

If Mike could find a way to reduce the problem for six hours a week between December 25th and February 28th at one ski lift, he would probably improve the customer satisfaction at his ski area by 50%.

Mike brought a team together to address this problem. Fran was a part of that team. The team suggested entertainment at the offending lift line during those crowded hours…clowns, jugglers, comedians, fiddle players, and more. The ski area did not have the margin of profitability to pay union scale for professional acts. But it did have a resource of amazing power. He had the power to give the entertainers free skiing in return for a few hours of entertaining at the lift lines.

This insight changed the quality of the experience for those of us who skied at Great Peak during those years. Were the customers startled? You bet!

Clowns, jugglers, and musicians gladly traded two hours of entertaining the crowds on the lift line for a day's pass on the mountain for their family. The line got no shorter, but it felt shorter and bad performers were as good as great ones. They made it a kind of a gong show. The distraction from the boredom of waiting was the key.

Oh, that's all right for a ski area, but it couldn't happen here.

Don't try to tell that to Fran Murphy. As a school superintendent, he was committed to delighting the customer. Owego, New York, at the time he became Superintendent, was a sleepy suburb of Binghamton, New York, itself a small city.

The community was divided between highly-skilled, largely white-collar IBM employees, and a much more diverse, largely blue-collar agrarian local population.

The children of the IBM parents took high-level courses in high school, went to college, and did pretty well. The children of the rest of the population were too often less successful. Instructionally, the problem was to raise the expectations, and the vision of this second

218

population, and to have everyone have fun doing it. This was attempted in many ways. We will highlight here just one of those efforts. As you read this, put it against your experience of attending school.

The local IBM plant wanted to help advance the cause of education, particularly in science and math education. They were active consumers of science and math expertise and would have liked to hire more local students after the students graduated from college. IBM had been very helpful to the school district in its efforts to move forward.

The vice-president in charge of the local plant was a very bright and capable man by the name of John Sponyoye. Fran had met with John several times. They had established a friendship. They had tried some projects together.

The projects had worked pretty well and they were now at a point to take some risks. Fran put together a team to focus on "raising the bar and delighting the customer". IBM had asked that the focus of these efforts be math or science. Fran insisted that this new initiative would take place, not just for the Owego School District, but for all of the Tioga County schools. The resulting effort was complex.

In the elementary schools, each teacher from grades three through six was given an ESTES "Eggspress" Rocket. These were designed to launch a rocket bearing an egg off a launch pad into the sky, where a parachute would open and the egg would be brought gently back to earth.

The rockets were about two feet tall. The teachers were shown how to assemble the rockets. (This is rocket science.) The teachers were engaged in the plan and were trained to implement it.

Each class, grades three through six would build a rocket. The custodians in each building would be trained how to launch them safely. The kindergarten, first and second graders would paint the rockets before the rocket engines were installed.

Each school would be given a device, which used a sighting protractor, and simple trigonometric principles, to measure the height of the rocket's path. The principal would be trained to work with sixth graders to gather this data. Half of the rockets in each school would be loaded with an egg. Half would be sent off "empty".

Every classroom k-6 would be asked to create a hypothesis to answer the question, "Which would go higher.... the one with the egg or the one without the egg."

The whole school watched the launch.

Each teacher would bring the data from their class to a county-wide conference on science and math teaching, where the data would be entered into a computer and a "Model" science experiment report in simple language would be generated.

The lab report would include the following sections:

Statement of the problem.

Hypothesis.

Method.

Materials.

Data.

Conclusions.

A copy of the lab report would be printed for each child.

For the remainder of the year, teachers would use this report format to work with the students on other scientific experiments.

The experiments the teachers would use would be provided to each elementary teacher, appropriate to that grade level's science objectives.

They would be labeled and packed in stackable Tupperware containers to cover the science topics at each grade level. These would be supplied by the consortium. Each summer, the consortium would reload the materials in the tubs and revise the teacher instructions based on faculty input.

At the conference, which was held for all of the teachers in the county, for all grade levels, Jim Lovell, Commander of Apollo 13 was the surprise presenter for the teachers of this rural and largely poor county.

Lovell held all the teachers spellbound as he first described the terrifying story of the Apollo 13 flight and then discussed how his childhood teachers had guided him to a love of science and math, and it was these early lessons that led to his success, in life, and on that mission. There was no way without IBM's help Jim Lovell would have been there. He was there that week to work with IBM on computer applications for space flight. We determine the date of his trip to Owego to line up with the day of the conference The schools just borrowed him.

The elementary teachers worked through the science kits that day in groups learning how to conduct the planned experiments. When they returned to their classrooms the kits were in place with instructions for use, waiting to be stored and used.

The high school and middle school Science faculty would meet that day with local IBM engineers who would answer questions about how the topics the teachers taught were actually used in the engineer's work.

In this way, the teachers could answer the common question from students, "How will I ever use this?" The other faculty met to consider how they could support the work of the science and math teachers using their non-science and math subject matter.

Bob Ballard, the oceanographer, who discovered the Titanic, spoke to all the assembled teachers in a live interactive video feed, later in the day from the Woods Hole Oceanographic Institute. He indicated that a decision had been made, that a teacher from the Owego Free Academy, Owego's only high school, would be traveling to Galapagos Islands to supervise students selected from the nation.

This teacher would be participating in broadcasts via a live satellite feed to each of the schools in the county, for two weeks covering the scientific expedition there. She would interview the scientists and share the

224

results of their work. There would be 5 broadcasts a day for the schools and/or citizens who could tune them in.

The results of the "Eggspress" experiment were announced. The lab reports were distributed to the teachers to bring back to their students as the day concluded.

Would that kind of experience change the way students looked at science? Would more students be more powerfully invited into science and math study?

Would those elementary teachers be more likely to do science experiments with their students?

Do you think the customers were delighted?

Is that how you remember school?

As you can see startling the customer is not business as usual. If it can be done in public schools, it can be done anywhere. We will share with you one more example from Fran's tenure in Owego about a public-school application using this critical principle, hoping that it stimulates a creative approach for you, in startling your customers with extraordinary service.

When Fran went to Owego, sadly, eleven students had died in each of the previous eleven years, one per year in incidents related to drugs and alcohol. Something needed to be done to change the culture among parents and students, to literally change the current expectations, which were that high school students would, of course eventually drink and would probably use drugs when they became adults, so why not begin now.

Most high school students did not know an adult who did not drink. And, they knew many who regularly even used drugs.

Fran had recently come from New Hampshire, as Superintendent of Schools in Conway. A small town in nearby Maine had lost a group of students in a car-train crash following their graduation ceremony. The crash had probably involved students and alcohol. The community had resolved to never let this happen again. They would create a non-alcohol graduation celebration, so compellingly that students would prefer to celebrate

226

together safely, rather than to use alcohol. Fran was aware of the efforts of that community when he faced Owego's problem.

In Owego, the biggest night for drinking and driving was the senior prom. The adult community in Owego loved its children. They were very willing to help. Fran approached the service clubs in Owego and found great support from the Rotary, Kiwanis, Elks, Zonta, and the Lions. To get students to participate in a post-prom, drug and alcohol-free celebration, powerful incentives were needed.

Because of financial contributions from the service organizations, and the county agency DWI reduction agency, Fran was able to offer a drawing at the end of the post-prom party. The items to be drawn included an automobile among other prizes, as an incentive to lure students to attend the event and forgo the traditional bad behavior, including the use of alcohol. With the help of the senior high PTA and a wonderful high school staff, an evening like no other was planned for the students.

A local university gym complex, complete with a

dance studio, a pool, racquetball courts, volleyball and basketball courts, was rented by the school system. Lifeguards and a DJ were hired. Students who wished to attend were required to travel from the prom to the event on a school bus (no bottles smuggled in) and had to agree to spend the entire night, enjoying each other's company, in safety.

The community cooked breakfast in the morning, and the students were released to go home, in the broad daylight. The last event of the night was the drawing which included computers, dorm-sized refrigerators, dorm size TVs, dictionaries, and the car. All of the seniors who attended won something.

When the event was offered to the students, initially they were slow to sign up. "My parents can't make me do this. It's my right to get drunk, and with any luck do other things, on my prom night," seemed to be the attitude of the students. One week before the event, however, there was virtually no one left among the student body to invite to a non-authorized private and drinking post-prom party. Virtually all students had signed up.

The adults who supervised the event were given a new paradigm. They could not stand around the side of the room in suits and dresses observing (snooper-vising), but were required to join in, swimming, playing basketball, and even dancing. The focus of the evening was to be entirely based upon fun. No corners were cut.

It was a night to remember. Fran wanted the kind of word-of-mouth advertising that would bring in the next generation of students the following year.

The story doesn't end here. The Chem-Free Prom Party that was offered in Owego was the first in New York State and was a huge success. School districts from across the State came to Owego to learn how to do it.

The New York State Assembly asked Fran to testify at a hearing in Albany. Fran did not go alone but brought two students and a local County official by the name of Ed Van der Mark to make the presentation.

On the way home, one of the students said, "I wish we could do this Chem Free Stuff, all year, instead of just one night." This trigged a new project in Owego, and some other school districts called the "Chem-Free Year". Here's the way that project worked.

Fran recruited some prominent local adults. From year to year, the adults changed, but this first year included the police chief, the mayor, a kindergarten teacher, the principal, a doctor, and others. Then he recruited some key students from the senior class. They included popular skateboarders, members of a garage band, the captain of the football team, the president of the student government, and cheerleaders.

Together with the adults and the students, Fran entered every senior classroom (focusing on English classes). He challenged the students in each classroom, "I am not going to drink or use drugs this year. Neither are the other adults and students standing before you.

I have $40,000 to spend to provide an outrageous trip or experience every month for those of you who choose to join me in this challenge. We will go skiing, probably more than once, and when we do the lift ticket and ski rental and lessons will be free. When you get hungry dinner will be provided... Those of you, who join us, will also be able to go to Toronto, or New York City, your choice, for the weekend and, well, you tell us what you want to do. We will try to make it happen."

"If you join, your name is going on a T-shirt, that you will be given, that will list all the members of the Chem-Free Project because we mean business. Everyone will know that you signed up. If you cheat, someone will find out. You will have to resign."

"Don't sign up if you don't want to do this. Don't worry about your parents. We are telling you before we are telling them. And, if, you want to tell them that that jerk, Murphy didn't let you know about it, and you missed the sign-up date, I'll back your story up.

Don't let anyone pressure you. We are hoping you don't join. I've got $40,000 to spend on fun events, and if you don't sign up, we are all going to Paris. If you do sign up, we won't be able to afford Paris, but I promise we will have an outrageous year together and your participation will be the stuff that legends are made of."

They signed up in droves. By and large, they kept their word. Subsequent unrelated surveys of student drug and alcohol behavior conducted by the State showed a dramatic decline in drug and alcohol behavior among seniors. When the seniors stopped using drugs and alcohol, younger students found it harder to obtain these substances. Surveys indicated that drug and alcohol behavior among all students began to decline when compared to previous years, and when compared to neighboring districts.

More importantly, the students and the volunteer adults had a blast. Fran and his team negotiated special rates for the monthly activities and the money went a long way.

Everyone remembers their favorite moment. For Fran, it was all 80 students together with the adult volunteers lying on their backs in the middle of a field in a giant circle, heads nearly touching, legs splayed out of the circle. in the darkest of nights.

The Catskill Mountains have little light pollution and, on that night, the blinding light coming from the milky way opened the opportunity to understand the meaning of a trillion stars. After a long while, the adults and students drifted back to their tents and cabins embraced by the croaking of thousands of tree frogs and the rippling sound of a lively creek bubbling with the frenzy of the melting of the last snows on the nearby mountains. What a moment!

Most importantly during the time of the project, which went on after Fran left, and for years after, Owego lost no more children to deaths related to drugs and alcohol.

Was the dramatic decline in at-risk behavior aided by the startling offer. Could it have been achieved by business as usual?

Drug and alcohol behaviors among people are not casual behaviors that are easily changed. To decide not to use drugs and alcohol, requires the same kind of personal reorganization as losing weight, or developing an exercise program, or turning a poor student into a scholar. The sub-text in both of these stories about the Chem-Free Projects is extraordinary customer service. We had to startle the students with extraordinary treatment that they did not, nor, could not, expect.

Schools do things on the cheap. ("We've got a field trip today to the museum. Bring two dollars for the bus, a dollar for the museum admission, and have your parents pack a sandwich.")

These projects would not have worked if students had to pick up the costs. They would not have worked if the meal provided did not exceed students' expectations. If the activity was bowling, and not skiing, students may not have done it. (Bowling is something they could do on their own.) If the site for the Chem-Free Prom was the high school gym, few would have attended.

Was Fran's thinking in the Chem Free year project substantially different from Chrysler's thinking, when they focused on cup holders. How important is it to delight the customer even when, as a public school system where most people believe there is little reason to exceed competitors?

If schools were to behave like this in all of the areas of their operation, what would happen to student performance? What would happen to taxpayers' support? What would happen to the morale of the staff? Could charter and other private schools recruit large numbers of potential students?

Organizations have to work hard to startle their customers with customer service. It almost always requires a team. The solutions are typically "out-of-the-box" and the work, when done well, makes a company, a store, a school, a government agency, a hospital, a military unit, or a church legendary.

Great leaders have three common characteristics: grace, legacy, and vision. If you have the vision to startle your customers with the quality of your service and the grace to do it with style, your legacy will be assured.

Be sure the improvements you are making add value from your customer's point of view.

This is a simple step. We need to remember to do it. When Chrysler began to advance the cup holder, they had a good idea. My minivan has at least eight. When does an optimal number of cup holders become "trans-optimal"?

The President of the Smithsonian Institute wrote a thought-provoking article in the Smithsonian Magazine about ten years ago. He talked about "trans-optimal" technology. His example was the wristwatch.

The first watch was essentially a clock you could carry in your pocket. It wasn't very different from other spring-wound clocks except in its size.

Unfortunately, the glass crystals covering the face of the watch would often break. So, someone invented, what was called the "Hunter's Case", which incorporated a metal cover that would spring open to allow you to see the time. This worked pretty well.

When the Industrial Revolution and mass production began to dominate manufacturing in the early 1900s the pocket watch became less useful. The assembly line worker couldn't take time from his drill press to retrieve the watch from his pocket, pop open the case and read the time.

The wristwatch achieved popularity. The worker could turn his or her wrist, look down, and know the time without interrupting work. During World War one the wristwatch was so popular among soldiers that it became something that nearly everyone had or wanted.

With the advent of solid-state technology, the wristwatch changed again. The highly accurate mechanical watch became even more accurate when it became operated electronically. For an inexpensive price, a person could buy an electronic wristwatch whose face was black. If the person pressed the button, the face of the watch would light up with a set of red numerals indicating the correct time. These were LED watches.

The President of the Smithsonian Association immediately knew that this technology would not last. The watches were cheap and reliable but he knew that, with this technological advance, we had gone beyond the optimal functioning of a wrist watch, and walked it backward. It now took two hands to tell the time, again. This was a new dinosaur looking different. It had some of the same weaknesses as the "railroad watch" with the hunter's case.

Not all advancement is advancement. You can bring a product to the point where the enhancement decreases the effectiveness of the product.

Would 12 cup holders be helpful in a seven-passenger van? If you could include a cup holder in the headrest, would you want it there? We shouldn't guess at customer requirements, needs, or desires. We should test the market. Service enhancements are not service enhancements unless the customer would want them.

Customer service behavior also involves the case of resolving conflicts with customers. How do you use the "test" concept in resolving customer problems? This, too, is pretty simple. The danger here is that, if you neglect this step, you may fail to resolve the problem.

Sid loves to go to Romano's Macaroni Grill (they have great customer service). One time, we were dining together at the Macaroni Grill. Sid had ordered their lobster ravioli. They were out of the product. The waiter was great. He apologized. He made suggestions for a tasty alternative. Sid made a second selection, but not without grumbling a bit.

We were done with our meal and dessert was in the air. Sid loves Macaroni Grill's Tiramisu. He ordered it. The waiter indicated that he regretted having to say this twice in one day to a customer. But they were out of it, as well. It was college graduation weekend in Rochester. The crowds were huge. He was sorry. Sid ordered coffee instead.

Minutes later the manager came over to apologize again. He indicated that he had heard the whole sad story and he was prepared to offer Sid any item from the dessert menu free of charge as an apology for his disappointment. Sid said," You don't have to do that. I am all right."

Sid doesn't like anything else on the dessert menu.

As we left the restaurant, we realized that this very well-meaning manager had caused himself a bigger problem, than what he had, when Sid was talking to the waiter.

Sid had resolved his problem with Macaroni Grill.

When the manager offered something special, Sid was forcefully reminded that he was probably owed some compensation for the twin disappointments that evening. Then, what he was offered was something he didn't want, and, therefore, for the first time that evening, he had felt he had been wronged.

It is a mistake for us to assume that we know our customers well enough to know how to compensate them for any damage or loss they may have experienced. We always have to "test" our solution on the customer before we roll it out.

This should not be confused with a negotiation. Let me show you in the following example what the manager could have done. Then I will show you how it might have become a negotiation, which is not in the best interest of the restaurant.

"Sid, do you like other items on our dessert menu?" the manager might ask.

"Not particularly," Sid might reply.

"Let me offer you a certificate for tiramisu for the next time you come in. I am going to write right on this, that if we are out of tiramisu the next time, I will make it double or nothing. If we are out tiramisu then, you will get both a free dessert and the dinner will also be on the house," the manager might add.

That was done right. The manager checked to see if he could solve the problem now at the price he was willing to pay, if he couldn't, he already knew Sid loved the tiramisu. He could just offer a future opportunity to enjoy it.

Here it is done poorly, as a negotiation:

"Sid, I like to make this up to you. Would another dessert on the menu be all right?" "No", Sid might reply.

"How about a free dinner?" The manager might ask.

"No."

"How about my first-born child? A new Mercedes?

A Lear jet?"

You don't ask the customer how much they should be compensated for the loss they have experienced. You ask them which $3.95 choices they would prefer.

This is how you test to make sure your resolution to a conflict with a customer is satisfactory.

Questions:

1) Can you think of a time you were startled by an act of exceptional customer service? What was your reaction?

2) Are you loyal to companies that greatly exceed your customer service expectations?

Chapter 17

Humor Can be
an Asset to
World-Class
Customer Service.

"A sparkle in the eye is essential to make humor useful in resolving customer disputes."

As we have already stated, diffusing difficult situations, with angry customers, using a reframing approach, requires a sparkle in one's eye. The reframer must display that they are in on the joke. They must be seen as kind. Sid has a great, positive, personality and he rarely is a problem customer, but, all of us have our moments.

One time Sid was in a difficult situation in a health care environment and he had "lost it". The nurse got a big grin on her face, reached over, and pinched one of Sid's ample cheeks.

"Aw, poor baby," she said laughingly.

The comment was riskier than Most of us would want to be. Her laugh allowed this comment to work. It could not and would not have worked otherwise.

One time Fran was facing his administrative team in a heated meeting. They were upset over a decision Fran had made. The argument was hot and not getting any cooler.

Fran seized an imaginary arrow in his chest and pulled it out wordlessly. He threw it on the ground and dead-panned, "You got me!"

The laughter defused the crisis and allowed a healing conversation to begin. Often what works to deal with customers in a problem situation, can work for you as a customer.

Recently, Sid was going to a hotel after a very busy day. He had reserved a non-smoking room. When he called the desk on his way to the hotel, they told him there had been an error in the computer, and, they had reserved him a smoking room instead. He was not happy.

When he arrived at the hotel, Sid left his bags in the car, and burst through the double doors in the lobby, looking over his shoulders furtively.

"Young lady," he spurted urgently to the reception clerk. "Forty-three customers are just climbing off my bus in the parking lot. They are tired. They are hungry. And, my, oh my, are they irritable."

"Forty-three people....?" the clerk inquired mouth agape.

"Well, it is forty-four when I am included. We reserved a room for me, too. Now, they all wanted single rooms and are all non-smoking. I've got the reservation receipt right here." He fumbled through his briefcase.

"But ...", she stammered mid panic.

"Just kidding." Sid smiled.

She laughed, relieved that she was not going to

have to find rooms for forty-four, hungry, tired, and irritable people. This drama introduced by Sid was a real high point in her evening. She would tell the story again and again. It was a high point in an otherwise dull shift.

"Now that you have the news that you are not facing that horrible conflict, can't you find me just one non-smoking room?" Sid asked. "I am tired, irritable, and hungry. Look how easy this problem is. There is only one of me, not forty-four."

The desk clerk placed Sid in a suite, at no additional charge, that was non-smoking.

His originality and humor got him something that he would not otherwise have gotten.

This situation with Sid started with the caution that he was facing a difficult situation with this clerk. It went through the understanding that she probably had a few high-end rooms in reserve. He startled her with a fresh approach.

In this case, he was only going to get one chance to

resolve this problem, so the only test he could employ was to test this in his mind. Then he rolled it out with originality and humor.

To some people, reframing seems a little like teasing. It is simply a way to help people find their common humanity in a

tense situation. All of us have had the problem of a computer glitch that has caused us to miss an opportunity.

If we can find the humor in it, and nestle together in our common experience, we probably find a way to treat each other well, even in a difficult situation. The hotel clerk was just playing an old tape. It probably ran something like this: "Those fools in data processing, can't they get anything right. Here is another angry customer. I hate this. I am going to have to disappoint him again. This job stinks. I will just have to grin and bear it.'

When Sid reframed the problem, she began to see Sid differently and the problem differently. She appreciated the humor and was willing to "go to bat" for this guy who treated her the way her older brother does. It is this last point that makes it seem a little like teasing someone but in a kind way.

There is power in this model. People who use it break down the barriers between "us" and "them". When those barriers disappear, the "us" and "them" become "we". When it is just, us, we can usually resolve the problem.

Let's use this model, one more time with a customer service application.

A long time ago Johnson and Evinrude Motors manufactured a device that was used for skin diving. It was a floating gasoline-powered compressor unit that pumped air through a twenty-five-foot-long hose to the diver below. Johnson called theirs the air buoy unit.

The units were discovered to be defective and dangerous. Sooner or later the exhaust manifold would crack and exhaust would seep into the air intake.

Fran bought one used. He had been using his device for about eight years when the exhaust manifold cracked.

Smoke from the engine began to enter his face mask. It could have put his life at risk. He did not know about the issues with the design. When he brought it to be repaired, the shop told him they could not repair it. The company would not permit it. These devices were too dangerous.

In those days, there was no other remedy. Johnson and Evinrude were not compelled to make it right. And, they did not. The only option available to the dealer was to suggest to Fran, the customer, that he take this relatively expensive piece of equipment to the curb. This was not a good answer from Fran's perspective.

The argument went on long and hard. There was no apparent solution in sight. In those days, the dealer had few options to address the problem. Finally, the dealer said in frustration, "All right, I'll replace it. I'll give you an equivalent value to this product in pounds of arsenic."

"What would I do with arsenic? It would kill me," Fran muttered.

"Ah-Ha", the dealer smiled. "You are beginning to catch on." I can't use that broken machine either. We are both victims here.

This did not completely resolve the problem, of course, but, at least both parties shared one common insight and had enjoyed some laughter together, which, was not a bad beginning.

The approach of the dealer held within it the possibility of humor but came dangerously close to sarcasm.

Question:

1) Can you think of a time when humor diffused a tense customer service situation?

Chapter 18

A Fresh Approach
is Needed

"We must create startling new goods or services that reflect a profound understanding of our customer's needs, wants, and desires."

When designing customer service standards and expectations, originality is also important. People are not going to satisfy today's customers with the level of service they find all around them. Today's customers expect a fresh level of service, not a warmed-over approach borrowed from the company XYZ.

If you have done your research and you understand the customer's relationship or potential relationship with your product or service, you have the chance to create a truly original concept. Fran was Superintendent of Schools in Conway, New Hampshire.

During his time there, there were 7,500 residents; yet, on any given weekend, there could be 75,000.

The 75,000 justified a movie theatre, but the 7500 did not. The theatre there took a page from the ski area's playbook. The movie theatre was under-utilized during the week and packed on weekends and holidays. They offered a mid-week annual pass.

If people bought the pass at $200 a year per family or $100 per person, they could come as many times as they wanted, Sunday through Thursday except holidays. (They offered the passes for sale in November and December, to make it a convenient Holiday present.)

The movie theatre maximized the use of its mid-week capacity and increased revenues. They delighted the often low-paid residents of the valley, who could suddenly afford to go to the movies frequently. It was a "win-win".

Originality was a natural out-growth of the understanding developed about its customers. Residents loved the pass. This kind of originality often delights the customer.

The following is an example of what reframing is not:

Thank God, it was an unseasonably warm day when a timid young Alice signed up for a ski lesson with Sven.

It took 20 minutes to help Alice put her ski boots in the binding on the skis. (It usually took 2.) It took five unsuccessful trials for her to finally master getting on the ski lift to go to the top of the easy slope. Her immobility at the top of the hill lasted another twenty minutes and it took her two hours to come down the first 400 yards.

Another ski instructor flashed by Sven and Alice while they paused at the top of the hill to start their second run.

"That's what I would like to do!" Alice said hopefully.

Svan replied, "When pigs fly!"

He thought he had reframed the situation. What he

had done, of course, was to use his old habit of sarcasm, but he called it reframing.

Reframing is aimed at a "win-win". When reframing has been done successfully, both sides are smiling, feeling happy, and positive, a problem has been put into a new context. There is some relief that both sides will not have to wallow in a difficult problem. Clarity has been gained from ambiguity.

When someone tries to "win", tries to put someone else down, using sarcasm reframing never succeeds, and in fact, can bring a negative reaction.

Reframing should never be designed to defeat the customer.

Any new behavior is risk-taking behavior. Repeated patterns of behavior tend to bring predictable results. If someone is accustomed to using a snow shovel to shovel their driveway, they pretty much know what to expect. They know how long it will take. They know how stiff their back will be when they finish. They know how high the piles of snow will be after they shovel the snow. They can even imagine how heavy each shovel will be.

If you buy a new snow blower, all that predictability goes out the window. You will not be able to reliably predict anything about removing the snow for a while.

The snow blower will be a great improvement eventually, but you are taking a risk. Predictability builds confidence. When things are predictable, they are reliable. When they cannot be predicted they are unreliable.

Most of us would view the new snow blower as a plus. But there is some risk in changing.

All change requires some level of risk. Bobby Kennedy said, "Change is not neutral, change has enemies." He also said, "no one likes change, except a wet baby."

To try reframing, we need to try out new behaviors. Sid and Fran can use reframing with less risk. They have been doing it for years. There is a significant risk with reframing. If you try to use reframing and you dip into sarcasm, your customer will see your behavior as confrontational, and their tendency to be defensive will increase. You need to be optimistic with a sparkle in your eye to reframe safely.

Exercise is a good way to think about this. We don't encourage people to jump right into reframing with customers without any practice. Just like in exercise, you should start slowly, safely, and increase, as your "muscles" get stronger. Here are some practical suggestions of how to begin, and how to grow in your ability to reframe safely:

- Begin using reframing as a customer. The people you are doing business with can't afford to punch you in the nose or holler at you if it goes badly. They get paid to be nice to you. Therefore, these are particularly safe people to use to try out your new skills.

- Try it with your family and friends.

- Try the simple ones like a fresh answer to a simple question like "How are you today?"

- When you bring it to the workplace, try it first with subordinates and colleagues.

- When your colleagues discover what you are doing, role-play with them how you might use it to deal with difficult customers. Practice until everybody agrees you have got it right.

- When you are feeling comfortable, reframe some issues for your boss.

- Now you are ready to try it on your customers. Begin gently. Watch for feedback. Expand your risk-taking, as you find success.

If you have done it right, people will find you to be a humorous person, with a fresh perspective. They will think their experience with you has been fun. They will tell others, that you "Made their day"

Why would we bother to "roll it out"? The truth is

that despite all this talk about a service economy, the expectation for customer service is steadily rising while service itself is disappearing.

Our encounters with businesses today inevitably bring us disappointments. More and more restaurants expect me to get my own food and bus my own tables. Nearly gone are the knowledgeable department stores and hardware stores where true experts would talk knowledgeably about the products and offer solid advice before purchase.

What we find instead are warehouses with cash registers.

Shoe stores, for example, used to be places that measured your feet and brought you their products to try. Now you are faced with an acre of shoe racks and a cash register.

**Customer service seems to be
at an all-time low.**

The approach to customers today, too often, also fails to meet the mark. Customers get into our faces. We fall into comfortable, defensive patterns. The situation escalates, and everyone goes home with elevated blood pressure, unhappy.

We need to rethink customer relations at two levels. First, we need to focus on how we can delight the customer. How can our product or service become indispensable to our customers? How can we set a new standard for service for our customers that puts competitive products or services, at a competitive disadvantage? To do this, we must reframe our thinking. We must create startling new goods or services that reflect a profound understanding of our customer's needs, wants, and desires.

Second, we need to find a way to resolve the inevitable conflicts that will arise from the disappointments that our customers have in our goods and services. In order not to fall into the old traps of defensive behavior, we need to reframe these encounters to help our customers find our common interests and values. We

259

need to startle these customers with fresh approaches and embrace them with our concern and support.

Questions

1) Can you try these ideas in an environment that involves little risk?

2) Who is it that you can use to safely try out reframing?

Chapter 19

Motivation and Enthusiasm

Teachers often complain about unmotivated students. "If these kids were motivated to learn, I could teach them a ton." Employers often talk about unmotivated employees. "They are just plain not motivated to achieve excellence."

Fran told the teachers who complained about students, that the parents gave us what they had. They neither imported "bad" kids to torment us, nor did they keep the good ones at home. Our job was to educate all the kids in our town, whoever they may be.

Most psychologists agree that people are born motivated. Babies are motivated to eat. (Ask any nursing mother.) They are motivated to sleep, go to the bathroom, be held, etc. Curiously, motivational problems with children are not usually identified until they enter school. Perhaps the very tasks that students are asked to do in some classrooms squash native motivation.

"I was king of the hill, the apple of my mother's eye, leader of my chums until I met you, teacher, and all your words and numbers," a self-aware child might say. Some teachers pretend to teach while their students pretend to learn.

Others see sharing the skills knowledge and attitudes needed to thrive in a complex and often challenging world to be life's greatest privilege. Students lucky enough to study under this latter type of teacher are lucky enough. Fran always views the act of teaching as inviting students into the life of the mind.

Some teachers are demotivators, sadly.

A researcher named Seligman initiated a new

direction in psychological research that has helped us understand what happens to animals and people to cause motivational deficits.

Seligman was studying dogs in a cage with a shoulder-high barrier dividing the cage into two sides.

There was an electric grid under each side of the cage. In earlier experiments using the same apparatus psychologists studied how quickly animals learn to escape from punishment. (Aversive situations.)

A light would be lit on the wall of the cage and seconds later the side of the cage where the dog had been standing when the light lit would get a jolt of electricity. This was repeated until the dog learned to escape to the "safe side."

The good news for dogs in this kind of experiment is that dogs quickly learned to leap to the safe side of the cage usually in less than 15 trials, most much faster.

Seligman's experiment used the same equipment but was very different, and a bit crueler. He chained the dog to the unsafe side of the cage. He turned on the light repeatedly. The dogs could not escape and were shocked.

He then released the dogs to see if this exposure to aversive events from which they could not escape would lower their ability to learn to avoid the shock in the future. The question was, "Would being chained to inescapable shock inhibit the dog's ability to learn how to escape in the future when the dogs could move freely about the cage. After being released from the leash, the dogs had not learned to escape to the "safe side" of the cage even after 70 trials.

During the shock phase when the dogs were chained to the cage wall, the behavior of each dog formed no pattern. Some dogs defecated. Some dogs vomited. Some dogs shook. But whatever behavior the dog exhibited, they would continue that behavior each time the light went on instead of exhibiting behavior that brought them relief.

They had, it seemed, learned a "helpless behavior". After all, they did some behavior and after some time doing that behavior, the shock stopped. Was the dog inadvertently led to believe that what he did during the

264

shock was what caused it to stop? Was the researcher inadvertently rewarding the dog's behavior, making it harder for the dog to try a novel behavior, because the old behavior "worked"? That is why it is called learned helplessness.

The only way these "damaged" dogs could be taught to get themselves to the safe side of the cage when the light lit up on the wall, was to be dragged with long leashes to the safe side of the cage. The researchers had to drag them repeatedly until the dogs learned the pattern and moved on their own. It often took 70 trials to teach them what naïve dogs learned in less than 1 trial without being dragged to the safe side.

Even these repeated and coercive measures worked only when the barrier in the middle was removed. Seligman called the factor inhibiting the natural escape motivation by the dog, "Learned Helplessness."

Seligman said that when a person or an animal is placed in a situation where there is no alternative but failure, they sometimes learn that their own skilled behavior cannot get the results they seek. Their persistence at task declines.

There have been thousands of studies using people and animals that have confirmed this finding. Learned helplessness is a robust concept in the "new" psychology. It explains how we can destroy a person's initiative by repeatedly punishing a person with no opportunity for the person to get relief.

Imagine a child with an undetected vision problem being asked to learn to read. The child is chained to an inescapable aversive series of events. This is a recipe for both creating a person who will have no confidence in their ability to learn to read and also a child who may appear to be unmotivated generally.

The studies on people have been less cruel but very interesting. One psychologist asked students to do complicated academic work in an environment that had uncontrollable loud noise. There were three groups. One group was subjected to the noise and could do nothing about it. Another group had no noise at all. The third group had a button to push that they were told could lower the noise if they needed to. They were asked not to use it because it would ruin the experiment. (The button was not connected to anything. And none of them pushed it.)

The students in the third group with the button were given the same noise as the first group and were asked to do the same tasks as the other groups.

The first group, subjected to the noise with no possibility for relief, did poorly on their academic tasks. They were, after all, much like the dogs in Seligman's original experiment "chained" to an inescapable negative circumstance.

The group that had no noise at all, of course, did pretty well.

The surprise was that the group that thought they could control the noise (even though they couldn't) performed about as well as the group that had no noise at all.

One of the surprising findings by the psychologist in this experiment was that the students in the uncontrollable noise group also did significantly worse on

267

an unrelated academic test, back in their regular classroom, during the next week. It appears that the effects of being chained to a negative circumstance generalize to other non-related, life events.

In plain English, the facts are these, when people discover that bad things are going to happen to them and there is nothing they can do to prevent it, they become unmotivated and dysfunctional. (Learned helpless.) This probably should not surprise us.

When a loved one dies from a long illness, we find ourselves chained to a negative circumstance. No Psychologist is manipulating us. We try new doctors seeking second, and third opinions. We search the Internet for new medicines. We try feeding the loved one presumably healing diets. No matter what we do, the person dies. Here we are chained, just like in the earlier experiments, to an aversive event.

Our persistence at other tasks outside our mourning at least temporarily declines and we become a bit dysfunctional. Human reactive depression is the most common form of everyday depression. It occurs when we encounter bad events in our lives. Seligman holds it may be the same thing as Learned Helplessness.

The plain and simple fact is that unmotivated people are easy to find; we could if we wished, retool perfectly capable people to make more of the unmotivated ones.

We do. When a teacher demands that a student do something that they cannot physically accomplish, the student is likely to become learned helpless. An example might be demanding that a child with an undiagnosed vision problem learn to read.

If the teacher then punishes the student for failure, the teacher can manufacture a student who will carry a motivational deficit. This learned helpless attitude could last a lifetime and be generalized to other kinds of challenges. This is not overstated. Research supports this statement. Young minds are like freshly poured concrete. When you drop something on them, it often makes an impression.

We can harm employees and customers in the same

way. Perhaps the impact will not be as profound or long-lasting as it could be on children, at home, and in school. Yet, the impact will be longer-lasting and more profound than we might, at first, think.

An example of how an employer damaged the motivation of an employee happened recently in a store in the Rochester area. A night cleaner took a lot of pride in his work keeping "his" store clean. He often told people where he was a cleaner and asked if they had ever seen a cleaner store.

He had extensive experience in the janitorial field and was given a high-speed buffer to clean his floors. He knew that the high-speed buffer required a different kind of wax than they had been using. He knew this because of his previous experience working in other companies. He also spoke to the vendor from the floor wax company, and read the material that came with the buffer.

Some of his friends also worked as janitors. He knew his job.   He mentioned to his boss that the high-speed buffer, with the old product, would cause the floors to become milky or cloudy. The increased friction of the high-speed buffer would burn the old-style wax.

He was told, "We are going to continue to use the old product. It has always worked well for us."

He continued to raise the issue and continued to get the same feedback. He showed his supervisor the "milky" floors, and could not capture his boss's attention. As time went on, he began to take less interest in his work. The way he framed the problem was, "If they don't care how this place looks, why should I?"

The cleanliness of the store declined. The business declined. He was fired, because his boss said, "He is a lazy good for nothing." Eventually, the business closed. Even though a new cleaner temporarily improved the cleanliness of the building, the reputation of this food store had gotten so low that the customers never came back.

Employees are often paired with inescapable negative circumstances by bosses who don't listen. Most times, the employee is the greatest expert about their job. The secretary knows more about her job than the boss does. Why wouldn't the boss listen to the secretary, as she explains her need for additional equipment, materials, or training?

Customers, too, can be made dysfunctional. In ways that businesses don't often understand, the businesses establish relationships with customers. Many employees see customer encounters as events, not relationships. Yet for the customer, it is not a string of unrelated events, but a relationship.

Let us share an example. Dave owns and operates a barbershop in the Browncroft neighborhood in Rochester. He knows he shares a relationship with his customers. People who have lived in that neighborhood, sometimes, 20 years apart, can connect by laughing about their experiences with Dave, the barber. Dave is funny and warm. He never forgets a face or a person's story. His shop is filled with strangers who rapidly become friends caught in the embrace of Dave's laughter. Dave becomes so captured by the stories at his shop that every once in a while, the haircut seems secondary.

What is interesting is how David empowers his

customers to express their concerns about his service. A customer said, "David, I'm OK with this hair cut but my wife told me that it is ridiculous. She says it is shaggy on the right and short on the left," a recent customer said in the middle of a busy shop one Saturday.

"Did you get out of the chair before I was done? Doggone it, you are always doing that. Spin around here. Show these guys that haircut. What do you guys think?"

"I could never have done this mess, could I? Sit down in this chair. Let me finish this one up... and, next time, don't be in such a hurry to get out of here. Be sure to tell your wife what a jerk you are. Don't blame this one on the old David. And, next time don't be so quick to get out of here."

All of us in the barbershop knew that if we had a problem with a haircut, no muss, no fuss. He would fix it. He empowered us to raise our concerns with his work through his example. He showed us that this was a relationship where one could feel free to raise issues.

By contrast, there is a car dealership in that same

neighborhood that never makes a mistake. When the newly installed battery ran out of power within the first month, they asked the customer what he had done to it. When a car being serviced, was vandalized, in their lot, they said it was his problem. When the car would not start they first fixed X, and when the car still didn't start, they fixed Y, then Z. They charged for all three; they taught the customer to stop raising concerns. Having the prestige of working with them should be privilege enough. Some customers, however, simply learned to go elsewhere.

No customer will be an interactive customer sharing concerns and seeking improvements if they are chained to a hostile or non-responsive company. They will either quit complaining or they will leave. Both responses are fatal to a company committed to continuous improvement.

The same researcher, Martin Seligman, has recently published some very interesting new materials. He has been able to predict election outcomes based on the optimism of the candidates. He has been able to predict the winners of athletic competitions based upon the optimism of the players and coaches in newspaper accounts after their previous victories and defeats. The results of his research on elections show clearly what other research also reveals, that people are attracted to positive, enthusiastic, and upbeat people.

Try this. I am going to introduce you to two women. The first is Sally. The second is Mary.

Sally believes life is difficult. A frequent topic of her conversation is her aliments and her friends' ailments. She frequently complains about taxes, her children's teachers, the cost of living, and the government, no matter which party is in charge. Her instant response to a proposal for anything, from anybody, is to say no. She walks with a stoop and has fairly low energy. On the plus side, she is loyal, long-suffering, and is very interested in other peoples' tales of woe.

Mary believes life is good. She is always looking ahead to the next challenge and opportunity. She is full of energy. She seldom complains about anything. She likes to say yes to even hair-brained ideas whether or not they have any possibility to bring good results.

In the darkest of situations, she can find something to feel good about. She has little patience with other people's sad stories and always wants to do something new, get something done, and move ahead. She is very future-focused and doesn't like to spend a lot of time on the past.

OK, here is the challenge. You are going to Cleveland for a conference. The weather will be rainy. You are going to spend a lot of time with one of these two employees.

Mary or Sally. Who do you want to go with?

The fact is that 90% by the actual account of the people we ask this question to, choose Mary.

Enthusiasm and optimism make a huge difference to our customers, our colleagues, and our employees. (Even to the readers of this book?)

Optimism and enthusiasm are a choice. We all have about the same number of bad things that happen to us. (Sure, some of us have it a little tougher.) Generally, we were all born, established relationships, some of which succeeded and some of which failed.

We all lost friends and relatives to illness and death. We all had successes and failures and we will all have been sick.

We will all die. These are not the issues that make one person optimistic, and one pessimistic. Some of the most cheerful people that I know have been in wheelchairs, lost a limb, or have had cancer. The question is not how much bad stuff has happened to each of us. The question is how have we responded to it.

How much pleasure does misery brings us? Some people seem to revel in it. Do some choose to press the misery button more often?

Let's play it out. Imagine if, on Friday night, one of our parents was diagnosed with cancer. Imagine if, on Saturday night, one of our pre-teen children came home drunk. It is Monday. A customer calls on a phone. Will our lives be enriched by being gruff or unkind to that customer, or is there a possibility that by being extraordinarily helpful to the customer, our lives may be happier?

It is important to charge your batteries

At a meeting, Sid will often ask, "How many of you like herbal tea?" Not very many hands go up. Sid says that he understands. He says that he usually makes himself a cup of herbal tea in the morning when he is in the office.

People come by his desk and ask him, "Sid, you are going to drink that tea before it gets cold?"

Sid's response? "Nope."

The questioner often looks at him peculiarly.

"I am not going to drink this herbal tea. I don't like how it tastes. But I sure do like how it smells." Sid will say if pressed. Sid works at recharging his own batteries. So does Fran. You must as well.

Glasser, in his book <u>Reality Therapy,</u> contends that people beyond their obvious physical needs have four basic needs:

- They need achievement. They need to make or do things they feel are important.

- They need power. They have to feel that they can influence people, events, or things in their environment.

- They need affiliation. They need to belong, to love, and be loved. They have to feel that people around them care about them.

- They need fun. They have to be able to play, relax, laugh and enjoy.

If the organization won't permit or encourage people to satisfy these needs, Glasser says, they will find a way to do it themselves. Sometimes, they will solve it in a way that is hostile to the organization.

In an organization that does not permit play, (a

strict seventh-grade classroom, for example) people will find an opportunity to play, sometimes with sarcasm, sometimes in a malicious way, sometimes with vandalism. How are you satisfying your four needs? How is your organization encouraging people to satisfy these four needs?

Do you find an opportunity to play every day? Do you "play" with your customers, your colleagues, your bosses? Do you ever organize opportunities, where you work, to help other people play? Golf tournaments, song contests, boss look-alike contests, parties, hikes, and surprises seem to help some people. Could you recharge your customers and yourself with silly promotions and games?

Dave, the barber, could recharge himself and his customers by issuing clipboards and crayons with a challenge to draw Dave, the barber, as he looked in the '60s, and then show them a photo. The photo would reveal that this civilizer of men's hair once looked like an unkempt hippy.

**Play should be an important way
that we recharge our customers and ourselves.**

Achievement can recharge us too. For those of us who are bosses, we need to remember to share the credit we get from achieving a big goal. If the goal is credited to the boss alone in the report at the end of the project, then he or she is the only person who gets to experience the achievement.

It is the recognition that makes achievement worthwhile. Customers can be recognized for loyalty, their twenty-fifth visit, their good ideas, (cash prizes for suggestions realized), and other contributions. A jeweler we know gives particularly cheerful customers a card thanking them for making his day.

Affiliation can recharge people's batteries. Fran teaches his classes, at the college, that one of the most important tips to improve time management is to spend at least 15 minutes a day while at work with someone you genuinely like.

He has observed in his professional practice that when he makes it a point to do this each day, he is more energetic and focused and can accomplish more. Dave, the barber, will spend anywhere from eight to 20 minutes cutting a person's hair. When he is cutting the hair of someone he likes, and there is no one waiting in his shop, he will deliberately slow down and enjoy the time he is spending with the customer. It recharges him for the rest of his customers.

Power, too, recharges us. The funny thing about power is that the more you share it, the more of it you will seem to have. The boss who empowers her employees gets more respect from them. One boss we know said to one of her employees, "That's a very good issue that you have raised; I like the way you are thinking about it. I trust you to resolve it well. Why don't you go ahead and make the final decisions on that? Or if you would prefer for me to make the call, I will."

She empowered the employee. The employee derived a boost from her boss' confidence that gave her more energy that day. The boss did not abdicate. She delegated her authority.

We can do this with customers, too. Nothing is more empowering to a customer than to say, "Great suggestion, we will implement it next week."

People do have fundamental needs. Ignoring your customers' needs will cause an inappropriate expression of those needs somewhere else. Supporting the needs will provide a release from the cares at hand and a boost for the employee or customer.

One woman approached Sid after a seminar. She told him that she treats herself well every day. She puts out the good china when she makes tea for herself on a weekend afternoon. She does not anticipate company. She brings out the nice napkins. She does not put the teabag in the cup but prepares the tea in the "special" teapot that her mother gave her.

"That's nice," Sid remarked. "Why do you do that?"

"I have had some bad news recently," the woman replied.

"How is that?" Sid inquired

"I have a terminal disease. The doctors told me that there is not much they can do for me, except to put me in touch with people who could help me cope with what I am going through. I didn't use their experts. I just decided to treat myself well."

"Sometimes I wear that special nightgown" she continued, "that I had put away for a really special evening. Now I wear it just for myself. I pour a glass of wine and light some candles. I work hard on the little things. I am much more conscious of using the time well that I have left."

Our time on this planet has always been temporary. We rent our space. We didn't buy it. We don't have the luxury of knowing when our last day is. What are we waiting for? Why wouldn't we treat ourselves as a guest? Are we not guest in our own life?

Each of us needs to be fresh for ourselves, our children, our spouses or significant others, our friends, our

284

colleagues, and, oh yes, our customers.

Being fresh is not an accident. To be fresh we need to refresh. We should not rely entirely on others to be treated well. We should carefully manage our mood before we are told we don't have much time left.

Sid and Fran like good coffee. Spending the extra few dollars per pound or fifty cents per cup to have it done right is an important way for them to acknowledge their personhood, and refresh themselves.

All of us look forward to a vacation. Somehow, a whining customer is easier to tolerate the day before you leave on a vacation to Bermuda. But we can't go to Bermuda every week. How do we build for ourselves little mental vacations to refresh ourselves every day that we live? Could we learn from the woman who told Sid about her terminal disease?

If your contribution to your family, to your colleagues, to your business, to your customers has the potential to be worthy, then it is worthwhile to recharge your batteries. Do it for all the people you help or have the potential to help. There is far too little patience in our society today. It is easy with the stresses that surround us to be short with other people. Being kind to yourself helps you to be kind to other people.

When a person is hurtling down a hill at a high rate of speed, it is not a good time to be discovering where the brake pedal is. This is the time to learn what enriches your life and makes you happy; not when you are under peak amounts of stress.

Take the time now to make a list of those things you will do for yourself to help center yourself. Then do them. Do those things that delight yourself. Do these things for your family, your friends, your coworkers, and your customers. Now is not too soon.

Empathy should not stop at your front door. You must have empathy for yourself. Meditation is making an appointment with yourself. It is one way for people to get in touch with their issues and find who they are.

Unless you have your social/emotional life in order; unless you have your physical life in order; unless you have your intellectual/cultural life in order; unless you have your spiritual life in order; you will not have the kind of psychic reserves that are needed to give world-class customer service.

The reason they tell you to put the oxygen mask on yourself first, on an airplane if there is a loss of cabin pressure is that you can't help the child sitting next to you when you are unconscious. You must first attend to yourself before you can reliably and cheerfully assist others. Build the time into your life to stretch, relax, and refresh.

Just like in all exercise you should start slowly and safely.

We all want world-class customers

Sidney C Hurlbert was a highly successful businessman in the finger lakes region of New York. He led his employees to exhibit amazing levels of customer service. This led to huge success.

Area clubs began to ask him to speak to them. He explained how and why to give world-class service. Soon the calls to speak came from further away. Soon he had to give up running businesses and become a full-time consultant and speaker on customer service.

Email Sid at seminars@sidneychurlbert.com

Dr. Fran Murphy led schools as a Principal and Superintendent. After retirement, he trained educators and became a Professor and College Dean. His work with people has always stressed service.

Email Fran at ketchdoc@yahoo.com

This is their second book.

Made in the USA
Middletown, DE
26 January 2023